GROW A PLANT PET

Other plant books written by Virginie Fowler Elbert
(with George A. Elbert)

FUN WITH TERRARIUM GARDENING

FUN WITH GROWING HERBS INDOORS

PLANTS THAT REALLY BLOOM INDOORS

FUN WITH GROWING ODD AND CURIOUS HOUSE PLANTS

THE MIRACLE HOUSEPLANTS

THE HOUSE PLANT DECORATING BOOK

Books for young people by Virginie Fowler Elbert

POTTERY MAKING

EASY ENAMELING ON METAL

GROW
A PLANT PET

Virginie Fowler Elbert
Illustrations by the author

Doubleday & Company, Inc.
Garden City, New York

Library of Congress Cataloging in Publication Data

Elbert, Virginie.
Grow a plant pet.

Includes index.
SUMMARY: Discusses the selection and care of popular
indoor plants including African violets, cacti, snake
plants, tomatoes, and marigolds.
1. House plants—Juvenile literature.   2. Gardening
—Juvenile literature.   [1. House plants.   2. Gardening]
I. Title.
SB419.2.E4   635.9'65
ISBN: 0-385-11698-5 Trade
0-385-11699-3 Prebound
Library of Congress Catalog Card Number 76–56284

CONTENTS

GROW A PLANT PET

Chapter 1

A PLANT IS A PET

A plant is a real pet. It grows and changes from day to day. It needs the same care as a walking animal, a flying bird, or a swimming fish.

It has to be fed, given a drink of water, a special place to live in, warmth, and light. You will have to groom it by trimming off leaves or branches that grow too long, or plucking off dead leaves. As the plant grows larger, you will have to find a roomier place for it to stay. A lukewarm shower bath is much appreciated. Some plants look better if their leaves are brushed off with a soft watercolor brush.

Sounds just like all other pets, doesn't it?

Go to the nearest plant store, supermarket, variety store, greenhouse, or garden center, and buy a plant pet. It will grow and put out new leaves, and add a flower or two. Your friends will all admire it, and probably go out and buy one, too. Then you can trade "cuttings" to make new plants. See Chapters 7 and 8 for this trick.

A plant doesn't take up much room. It lives comfortably on a window sill, or hanging from the ceiling near a window, or planted in a small area outside. It never barks or cries, doesn't have to be taken for a walk. You can leave it alone for a week or even two weeks if you go away. Feeding is only once a week. And it can't run, fly, or swim away. It is an ideal pet.

When you start looking at plants in a store, you will notice that each pot has a name label stuck into the soil. There should be two names on the label, one a nickname or common name, and the other a botanical one, which is its real name. The real name is a Latin one, and that is important to learn, as more than one variety of plant can have the same nickname. Or one plant can have several nicknames, depending on the greenhouse and the section of country where it is grown.

Two of the plants described in Chapter 10 have several nicknames. *But* among these nicknames, they each have one in common—Mother-of-Thousands. One is the Piggyback Plant, and the other is the Strawberry Geranium. You can easily see that they do not look alike.

Lots of plants are easy to take care of, and are easy to find in the stores. When you buy a plant for indoor growing, always get a small one so that you can watch it grow larger. It's like getting a puppy or a kitten, instead of a full-grown dog or cat.

Some of the easiest plants to grow in outside gardens are the many varieties of plants which originally came from Mexico and South America. In the North, though, where the winters are cold, the plants can grow outside only in summer. These plants are called annuals, as they die off after the first heavy frost and have to be replanted from seed the next year.

PLANT STORE SHELVES. All varieties of plants are in a store. Some you'll know from this book, others will be new to you. See how many you can identify. (Three new plants. 1. Anthurium, 2. Philodendron, 3. Beaucarnea or Pony Tail Plant.)

When you look in a seed catalog, you'll find that the claims for plant color and growth are for the best conditions. Try out seeds which look interesting, but keep your own records from year to year.

Let's start with a list of indoor fun plants that will grow easily when you give them a good home. Beginning in Chapter 10 there is a picture of each plant with its nickname or several nicknames, and its botanical or real Latin name. There is a short description of each plant. Then, on the following page or two you will learn how to care for each special plant. You will find out how to water, feed, groom, transplant, and to make new plants from old.

This list and the drawings will also help you to identify the plants in the store if there are no labels in the pots, which is often the case.

The suggestions for outdoor plants are on pages 134 to 143. There are three easy-to-grow flowering plants, and one vegetable. The flowers are bright and numerous. The plants can take all the ups-and-downs of an outdoor climate.

Before buying any plants, walk down the display aisle of plants at the store and look for the easy-to-grow and fun-to-look-at ones listed in this book. This way you'll know what is being sold, the sizes, and the prices before you buy.

And before making your choice of plant, be sure of the light you can give it, and how much it really needs in order to grow. The next chapter will help you decide.

Chapter 2

PLANTS NEED LIGHT

Now that you're back from that first trip to the store to look over all the plants, what's next? Before bringing a plant home, decide where your pet is going to spend the day and night and whether it is to be an outdoor pet, an indoor pet, or both.

If you live where the winters are cold, then you can have plants outside only in the summer.

But a houseplant will be with you summer and winter. A tropical plant, which most houseplants are, is used to growing all year round where the air is warm. It often does not need bright light. Plants which grow in a jungle are used to being shaded by tall trees.

So let's start with a houseplant. Walk around the rooms in your house or apartment and look at all the windows. Find out if they face north, east, south, or west. Is there anything which really cuts off the light, such as a big tree, or another building? The next step is to decide which window you want to use, and which plant will do best in that location. Try your own bedroom first, as you may want your pet plant to be near you so you can watch it grow.

If your window faces south, and there are no trees or buildings outside the window, then you have the most sunny one of them all. The sun will shine through the window on clear days almost all day long. You can grow your sun-loving plant right on the window sill. If the plant needs less sun, put it on a table near the window away from the direct light.

Choose one of the following plants for your sunny south window:

AFRICAN VIOLET—*Saintpaulia*
CACTUS—*Mammillaria dioica* and *Cephalocereus senilis*
COLEUS—*Coleus blumei*
LEMON GERANIUM—*Pelargonium crispum*
MUSTARD—*Brassica alba,* and CRESS—*Lepidium sativum*
PALM—*Chamaedorea* and *Howea*
PURPLE VELVET PLANT—*Gynura aurantiaca*
ROSE GERANIUM—*Pelargonium graveolens*
SNAKE PLANT—*Sansevieria trifasciata*
SPIDER PLANT—*Chlorophytum elatum vittatum*
STRAWBERRY GERANIUM—*Saxifraga stolonifera* (*sarmentosa*)

MARIGOLD—*Tagetes*
PETUNIA—*Solanaceae*
TOMATO—*Lycopersicon*
ZINNIA—*Crassina*

For a west window which gets the sun in the afternoon, your choice will be:

6

AFRICAN VIOLET—*Saintpaulia*
ALUMINUM PLANT—*Pilea cadierei*
CACTUS—*Mammillaria dioica* and *Cephalocereus senilis*
CHINESE BEAN SPROUTS, Mung Beans—*Vigna radiata*
COLEUS—*Coleus blumei*
DIEFFENBACHIA
LEMON GERANIUM—*Pelargonium crispum*
MUSTARD—*Brassica alba,* and CRESS—*Lepidium sativum*
PALM—*Chamaedorea* and *Howea*
PIGGYBACK PLANT—*Tolmiea menziesii*
POLKA-DOT PLANT—*Hypoestes sanguinolenta*
PRAYER PLANT—*Maranta leuconeura kerchoviana*
PURPLE VELVET PLANT—*Gynura aurantiaca*
RED-NERVED FITTONIA—*Fittonia verschaffeltii*
ROSE GERANIUM—*Pelargonium graveolens*
SNAKE PLANT—*Sansevieria trifasciata*
SPIDER PLANT—*Chlorophytum elatum vittatum*
STRAWBERRY GERANIUM—*Saxifraga stolonifera* (*sarmentosa*)
SWEDISH IVY—*Plectranthus australis*
WANDERING JEW—*Tradescantia fluminensis* and *Tradescantia blossfeldiana* '*Variegata*'

MARIGOLD—*Tagetes*
PETUNIA—*Solanaceae*
TOMATO—*Lycopersicon*
ZINNIA—*Crassina*

An east window where the sun shines through in the morning means a choice of:

AFRICAN VIOLET—*Saintpaulia*

ALUMINUM PLANT—*Pilea cadierei*

CACTUS—*Mammillaria dioica* and *Cephalocereus senilis*

CHINESE BEAN SPROUTS, Mung Beans—*Vigna radiata*

COLEUS—*Coleus blumei*

DIEFFENBACHIA

LEMON GERANIUM—*Pelargonium crispum*

MUSTARD—*Brassica alba,* and CRESS—*Lepidium sativum*

PALM—*Chamaedorea* and *Howea*

PIGGYBACK PLANT—*Tolmiea menziesii*

POLKA-DOT PLANT—*Hypoestes sanguinolenta*

PRAYER PLANT—*Maranta leuconeura kerchoviana*

PURPLE VELVET PLANT—*Gynura aurantiaca*

RED-NERVED FITTONIA—*Fittonia verschaffeltii*

ROSE GERANIUM—*Pelargonium graveolens*

SNAKE PLANT—*Sansevieria trifasciata*

SPIDER PLANT—*Chlorophytum elatum vittatum*

STRAWBERRY GERANIUM—*Saxifraga stolonifera* (*sarmentosa*)

SWEDISH IVY—*Plectranthus australis*

WANDERING JEW—*Tradescantia fluminensis,* and *Tradescantia blossfeldiana 'Variegata'*

MARIGOLD—*Tagetes*

PETUNIA—*Solanaceae*

TOMATO—*Lycopersicon*

ZINNIA—*Crassina*

A north window has no sun at all, but there are many plants that will grow well in this spot. These are the plants that grow in the dim light on the floor of a tropical forest, such as:

ALUMINUM PLANT—*Pilea cadierei*
CHINESE BEAN SPROUTS, Mung Beans—*Vigna radiata*
DIEFFENBACHIA
PRAYER PLANT—*Maranta leuconeura kerchoviana*
RED-NERVED FITTONIA—*Fittonia verschaffeltii*
SNAKE PLANT—*Sansevieria trifasciata*
SPIDER PLANT—*Chlorophytum elatum vittatum*
WANDERING JEW—*Tradescantia fluminensis,* and *Tradescantia blossfeldiana 'Variegata'*

A room with a window that gives practically no daylight at all because of trees or buildings can still be a good place to grow and bloom plants if you use artificial light. Fluorescent light tubes are best. They are cool and will not burn your plant pet and they use less energy than an incandescent bulb. A desk lamp with one or two fluorescent bulbs will serve two purposes. You can study and read by it, and your plant can grow by it. Let the lamp stay on for ten or twelve hours each day. Or put two tubes into one shelf of a floor or wall bookcase. Your plants will become a lighted picture.

Your plant will flourish, even though there is very little sunlight in the room. *In this way you can grow all the plants on the list.* Under two tubes of fluorescent light the plants will grow better than on a window sill.

There are no cloudy days under the lights, as there are on the window sill.

Now that you have the light problem solved, you may still have trouble placing your plant at the window you have chosen. First, you will have to make sure the window sill is not too narrow to hold your pot and that a radiator top is not under the window. Then, decide if this is the window you will want to open occasionally for air. This is fine in late spring, summer or early fall, but your plant will freeze in winter. Tropical plants are allergic to temperatures below 50 to 60 degrees. If they were animal pets they would start to sneeze or shiver. The leaves of a plant will curl up, turn brown, and drop off in protest.

All these problems have simple solutions that are very practical.

Narrow window sill. Build a fold-away shelf. Attach folding brackets under the window sill, and add a board on top. Put screws through the holes in the brackets and up through the board. Cover the board with enamel paint to match the room. Or, if you use flat paint, cover it with a clear plastic varnish. Then your board will be waterproof, and you can wipe up any water stains, or soil from the pot. You might also try moving a small table or stool the same height as the window sill in front of the window and placing your plants on it.

1.

2

FLUORESCENT LIGHT. 1. A reading lamp with one or two tubes on your desk. 2. Two light tubes in one shelf of a floor or hanging bookcase.

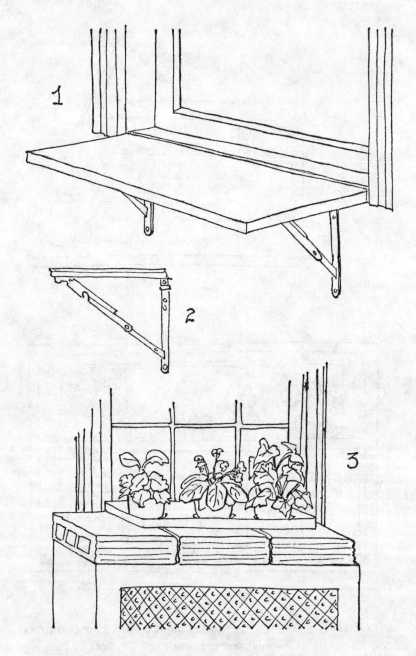

WINDOW SHELF. 1. Painted shelf with folding brackets attached to wall under a window. 2. Detail of folding bracket.

RADIATOR TOP. 3. Hollow building tiles on top of radiator cover. Tray holds the plants in their saucers.

Radiator Top. Put hollow building tiles or insulated building board on top of the radiator cover to protect the plants from too much hot, dry air. Then add a shallow plastic tray or aluminum baking sheet filled with pebbles and water on top of the tiles or building board. Stand each plant pot in a saucer so the plant will not absorb too much water. As the water in the tray evaporates it will keep the air around your plant moist and cool.

Open Window. You can always take the plant to another room when the window is open on a winter night. A permanent home in another room might be the best solution of all.

YOUR OUTDOOR GARDEN

Most of the annual flowering plants need lots of sun. Zinnias, petunias, and marigolds are all foolproof plants. Tomato plants, too, need a sunny place to grow. So pick a sunny garden space where neither house nor trees will shade the plants.

WORD OF WARNING: Do not buy your outdoor garden plant or put in seeds until you have read the next chapter on preparing the soil, and planting seeds.

On the other hand, with your detective work done on indoor light, you can now pick the right place for your plant to live. It's time to go back to the plant store and choose the indoor plant that fits your window sill light.

The next chapter will help you settle your plant into its new home.

Chapter 3

SOIL AND A POT TO GROW IN

You've picked out your plant pet and brought it home. It sits proudly on the window sill in the right light. Now what?

The first thing to do is to repot your plant in new soil made especially for houseplants. Even if your new plant looks all right now, it has begun to suffer. It probably received too little light and water in the store. It is up to you to give your pet the best possible care to get over the shock of moving from one home to another.

SOIL

As almost all houseplants are tropical, they are happiest in a loose and airy type of soil. In their natural growing area the soil lets a heavy rain run through but does not stay soggy. Yet, when the soil dries out, it is light and does not bake hard. In a pot the same action should take place. You'll match this condition by making your own *soil-less* mix, which is very easy. You only have to make enough for one pot at a time. The three parts you'll need are sold in small bags at plant stores, variety stores, garden centers, and in some hardware stores that carry garden supplies.

It might seem like a good idea to fill up the flower-pot with soil from the outside garden. It's a quick method, it doesn't cost anything, and plants grow in it outdoors. But the plants that grow in garden soil have been bred for a soil that is gritty and clayey with lots of small stones. The roots of the plants and trees spread over a wide area to get water and food. In a pot the roots of a plant are held in a small space and so have to have food and water easily available.

The plants which you buy are grown in a green-house, where they are planted in garden soil. There the conditions are very different than in a house. The air is very moist, so the soil stays damp and does not harden. The pots rest on long tables covered with pebbles which are moistened every day. Take out a teaspoon of that nice black soil and let it dry on a piece of paper. It will turn into a tan-gray gritty material. It is only the water which makes the soil look black.

There are some packaged *soil-less* mixes on the shelves of plant stores. Some are good, some are not so good. Ignore totally those packages labeled Potting Soil, or Humus Soil. They are just plain outside soil. You are going to repot the plant in your own modern formula of soil-less mix. It is the closest thing to tropical soil your plant will get, and it will love you for this change.

Let's start with the best for your new plant pet. You will need three separate materials for the mixture. These are sold in two- or four-quart bags. Buy one bag of *Peat Moss*, one bag of *Vermiculite*, and one bag of *Perlite*.

Here is the explanation of what each is, and what each does for soil.

Peat Moss is dried-out sphagnum moss. In the wet, spongy bogs where it grows, the old moss turns brown and packs down into a solid, deep mass of material. It is a dark-brown, lumpy fiber. Rub it between your fingers so that the lumps are broken down into a fluffy mixture. Do this before you measure out your formula. Peat moss supplies the solid weight and the organic matter for the soil-less mixture.

Vermiculite is made from the mineral *mica*. Lumps of this material are made up of thin, thin sheets of a transparent gold-tan material. The lumps are broken up and put into a furnace. The intense heat expands the sheets of mica. Out of the furnace comes a fluffy material of gold worm-like particles one-quarter to one-half inch long. All the fine little "plates" of each particle will hold water on its surface. This material both lightens the soil and holds in moisture.

Perlite is a volcanic material which looks like small-size white popcorn. It is light and helps to separate the mixture and lets in air.

Now you are ready to prepare your mix. First, put a cupful of each of the three materials into a bowl and

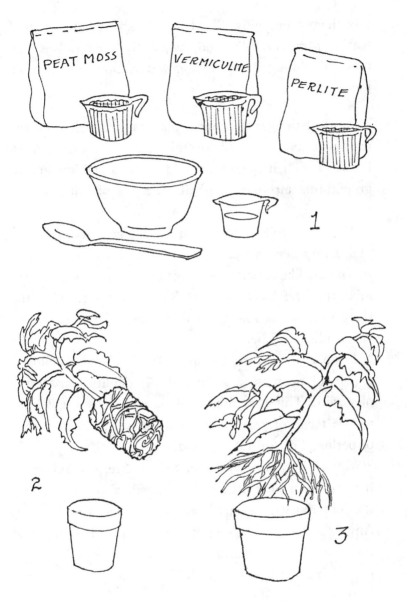

SOIL-LESS MIX. 1. Bags of material and cups showing amount needed, plus mixing bowl and one-half cup of water. 2. Pot-bound plant showing a net of roots. 3. Roots loosened and ready to be repotted in larger pot.

mix them thoroughly. Slowly stir in about half a cup of water. Mix carefully and, when the material is just moist all through, stop adding water. Don't get this soil too wet!

Most of the green tropical plants like a rich *acid* soil, and peat moss is good for this. But some like a *lime-like* soil. Then you will add half a tablespoon of ground-up, uncooked eggshells to a pot of soil-less mixture.

The basic soil mixture can be changed to suit those plants that need a richer soil. It can also be changed to suit plants like cactus, and other types which need a *lean* mixture. The basic mix is shown as 1-1-1, with the three parts always being in the same order—peat moss, vermiculite, and perlite.

For a rich mixture, the formula would be as follows: 3 cups of peat moss, 2 cups of vermiculite, and 1 cup of perlite. This rich mixture is 3-2-1. A lean soil mixture is 1 cup of peat moss, 2 cups of vermiculite, 2 cups of perlite. The formula is 1-2-2.

You can use any container to measure, depending on how much or how little soil you need. You can measure the material with a small can, a jar, even a tablespoon. Any left-over soil mix is put into a plastic bag and tied up to use again when soil is needed. Be sure that you put a label on the bag with the formula.

There are other materials which are used in formulas for special plants.

Bird Gravel is a fine gravel, or a very coarse sand—depending on the way you look at it. It is very good in a cactus mixture in place of vermiculite.

Milled Sphagnum Moss is not to be confused with peat moss. Milled sphagnum moss is fresh moss which has been freshly dried, then ground almost as fine as dust. It is light tan in color. This is used to cover planted seeds to help the young seedlings grow up strong. Otherwise, they might just go limp and fall over.

POTS

The next choice to make is the right pot for your plant. A plastic one is better in the house than a clay pot, as it holds more moisture in the dry atmosphere. Since the bottom holes are small you do not have to waste space with pebbles in the bottom for drainage. This use of broken-up clay pots or pebbles in the bottom is an old-fashioned idea. It was needed in greenhouses with the damp growing-benches, and pots filled with heavy garden soil which did not drain rapidly. Now the whole pot can be filled with soil so you can use a smaller pot.

If you want to use a decorated pot without a drainage hole, put a layer of pebbles in the bottom. Then put your plant in a regular plastic pot with a hole and put this pot inside the decorated one. This way, if you pour too much water on the plant, you can lift out the inner pot and throw away the extra water.

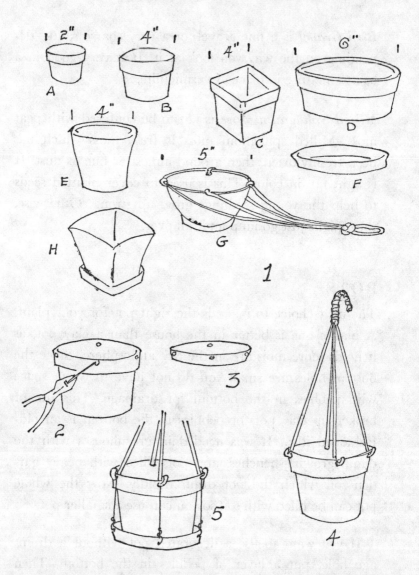

POTS. 1. Several sizes and shapes of plastic and clay pots: A & B, round pots, clay or plastic; C, square plastic; D, shallow azalea or bulb pot; E, rimless clay pot; F, a saucer; G, hanging pot with saucer; H, pot with attached saucer. MAKING A HANGING POT. 2. Holes made with a hot nail. 3. Saucer with matching holes. 4. Heavy wires in place. 5. Saucer held to pot by thin wires.

Use a clay pot if you have a tall, heavy plant which needs the weight of the pot to keep it from tipping over. Some cactus plants do better in clay pots as the soil stays drier.

Never put a plant in too large a pot for its size. It gets lost and spends all its time growing roots, and none growing leaves! Some plants will only flower when they are *pot-bound*. A pot that is too large holds too much wet soil. The plant will receive too much fertilizer for its size, will get indigestion, and the leaves will turn yellow.

When repotting you may put the plant back into the same pot, or you may need one which is one size larger. If, when you take the plant out of its pot, the roots are exposed all around the outside edges of the soil, then the plant is pot-bound. You'll need a larger pot. But if there is plenty of soil in the pot, and the roots are small, replace the plant in the same pot if it is plastic. If it is clay then you can match the size with a plastic pot.

Both plastic and clay pots are measured across the top width for identification—two-inch, three-inch, four-inch, and so on. The measurements may vary by as much as a quarter of an inch or so.

You will also need a plastic or rubber plant saucer to fit your pot, to keep the water from running out over window sill or table when you water the plant.

HANGING POT

Pots for hanging plants are sold with their own saucer

attached to prevent water from dripping on the floor. The hanging support of wire, chain, or rope is sold separately.

You can easily make your own hanging pot combination. All you need is a plastic pot and saucer, a large nail, pliers, wire cutter, coat hanger wire or heavy cord, and fine wire.

First, you'll have to make three holes in the rim of the saucer, and matching holes around the top edge of the pot for the wire to go through. Mark the spots with a pencil. A hot nail works well to make these holes. So, hold the nail with the pliers over a medium-to-low flame on your stove. Be sure you never touch the nail directly because it can get very hot. With the point of the hot nail, melt three evenly spaced holes on the top rim of the pot at your pencil marks. Reheat the nail, then press the nail point to the marks on the saucer.

Now that you have made the holes, you're ready to attach the hanging wires or heavy cord. Cut three pieces of heavy wire or cord to the length you want. Next, attach each piece to a hole in the pot. Twist the three loose ends of wire together with the pliers, and form into a hook. If you are using cord, tie the three loose ends into a strong knot.

The final step is to attach the saucer to the pot, using the fine wire. Cut three even lengths that will be long enough to extend from the holes in the pot to the holes in the saucer, plus extra for fastening. Pull each wire through its hole in the saucer, and twist the lower, loose end to the wire. Then, put each wire through a hole in the top of the pot. Pull the wires tight, so that the saucer is held snugly against the bottom of the pot. Tie the free ends by twisting around the main wire.

Your hanging pot is ready to be filled with soil and a plant.

REPOTTING

You now should have your pot and saucer, the soil mixture, and a tablespoon for scooping up the soil laid out on a piece of newspaper. Fill a bowl and a drinking glass with lukewarm water and you are ready to begin.

First, spread the fingers of one hand over the top of the pot. Support the stem with a finger on either side. Upend the pot. If the soil and plant do not slip out easily, tap the edge of the pot against the edge of the table. The plant should be away from the table top, hanging down in open air. Be careful that you do not bruise the plant.

Very gently swish the dirt ball in the bowl of water. Wash off all the old, gritty soil from the roots. Work quickly as roots do not like to be in the light too long.

Put about an inch or so of soil in the bottom of the pot. This amount depends on the size of the root ball, and the size of the pot. Set the plant in the pot with the roots on the soil. Add more soil to the pot, being sure that there are no empty spaces to hold air. Bring the soil up

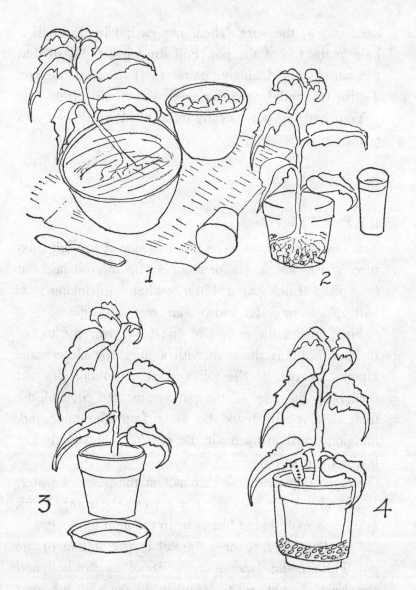

REPOTTING. 1. Washing off roots in lukewarm water. Bowl of soil-less mix and tablespoon ready. 2. Plant in new pot with roots spread out on mix. Water in glass. 3. Plant and pot ready to be put in saucer. 4. Cutaway drawing, showing pot inside another decorative pot instead of in saucer.

to the same level on the stem of the plant as it was in the old pot.

Press the soil down lightly, but do not pack too hard. Water well with lukewarm water until it drains out of the bottom holes. Tap the bottom of the pot lightly on the table to settle the soil. Put the name of the plant on a marker, and stick it in the pot.

Put the pot in its saucer, and place it back in its new home. With this method of transplanting each new plant as soon as you buy it, you will find that you have a green thumb, not a brown one.

YOUR OUTDOOR GARDEN

You'll want to grow simple plants at first. They should be hardy plants that can take rapid changes of climate, and not suffer too much. Start with a small area for your first garden. This way you can watch the growth of the individual plants, and really take care of them. Once learned, you'll know how to handle a larger garden next year.

You've picked your place in the sun, about five feet square. With a shovel, dig down to the full depth of twelve inches. If this area has not been used for a garden before it will be full of old weed roots and stalks. As you loosen the soil with the shovel, and before you turn over the clod, reach down and pull out any weeds you find. Shake off the soil and throw stalks and roots into a pile beside your working area. Turn over the clods of dirt so that the bottom is on top. Repeat all over the bed.

Sprinkle fertilizer all over the turned over soil. See Chapter 5 for the right fertilizer to use.

Next, go to work with a hoe, breaking up the lumps by chopping, and pushing, and pulling until the area is level. If you do not have a hoe you can use the shovel to break up the lumps.

The final smoothing is done with a rake. Go over the garden with a steel rake, pulling out stones, breaking up any lumps left by the hoe. Remove any last bits of weeds or roots remaining in the soil.

The next step is to plant your garden.

If you have chosen seeds, then they have to be planted early in the spring. Check the seed packages for the right planting date for your part of the country. Plan where the seeds are to go, placing the lowest plants in front, highest in the back. Or use the low plants for an outside border, with the tallest plants in the center.

Make a shallow, half-inch-deep line by drawing your index finger along the top of the soil. Sprinkle seeds down the length of the line, with four inches between the seeds. The farther apart the seeds, the less thinning out you'll have to do when the plants come up. And there will be less disturbance of roots in the thinning-out process. Push soil over the seeds, and pat down lightly. Put a marker at the end of the row, with the name of the plant attached.

Fill up the whole bed, leaving about ten to twelve inches between rows.

When all the seeds have been planted, sprinkle the area with a fine mist of water, using the spray nozzle on the hose, or a watering can. A heavy stream of water will wash the seeds out of the soil.

The garden bed is prepared exactly the same way if you are going to put in plants. Plants, though, are put into the soil much later than seeds. You'll know the right date for your part of the country when flats of small plants like petunias, zinnias, and marigolds appear in the garden center or plant store. Tomatoes are always put into the garden as plants, usually around the end of May when the ground is warm and the nights not too cold.

Each plant should have enough space around it to grow, as outdoor plants do not like constant replanting. Their roots are not confined to a small area. They grow deep, and far out into the soil around them, tangling with each other. Leave about eight inches between each plant.

As each plant is put into the hole you have dug for it, pour in enough water to settle the roots, then fill up the hole with soil. Once all the plants are in the soil, water the garden with a fine mist from the hose or watering can.

This is a good time to start your garden notebook. Enter the name of each indoor or outdoor plant. Then

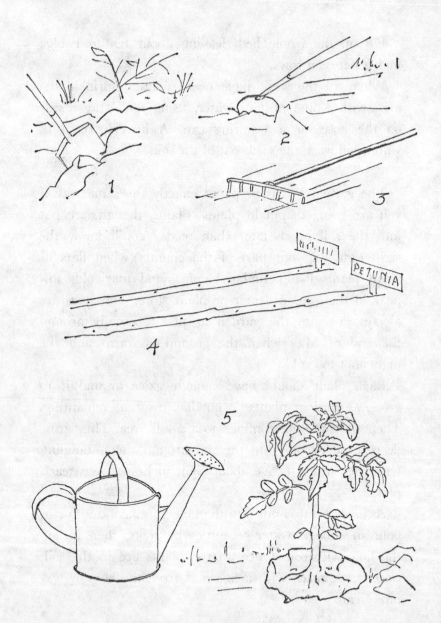

YOUR OUTDOOR GARDEN. 1. Turning soil with a shovel. 2. Breaking up lumps with a hoe. 3. Smoothing soil with a rake. 4. Planting seeds in rows. 5. Large watering can has a fine spray head at the end of the spout. 6. Putting a tomato plant in the ground.

include where they were bought and the cost. Measure the size of the top of the original pot. For outdoor plants, make a plan of the garden. Also measure the height of each plant.

From this time on, enter when the plants were watered, fed, and transplanted. Make note of the growth in new leaves, branches, and height. Indicate when trimmed, how much new growth resulted and how soon. Always include dates. You can also add the amount of sun or shade your plants are receiving each day, and in which direction your window or outdoor garden faces.

Now that both indoor and outdoor plants are in their right soil and pots, they are going to need watering. They, like any pet or human, need water to stay alive. And it is up to you to provide the right quantity at the right time.

Chapter 4

PLANTS NEED A DRINK
OF WATER

Most plants grow best when the soil around their roots is moist. When it dries out too much, growing stops and the leaves begin to droop. Rush to the rescue with water, and the leaves will quickly recover. Soil that is too wet will keep the roots from getting oxygen (like drowning). The roots will rot and cut off the food and water supply from the plant. Leaves and stem will go soft and mushy.

It takes awhile to learn what is too little, what is too much, and how and when to water each plant. Don't be discouraged if your plant dies. Even the best of professional growers have this happen to them. It is part of learning what suits each plant. Just go out and get a new plant, and then follow a different routine of watering, according to your record book.

The amount of watering also depends on the season of the year.

In the summer, when the air is very humid, some plants may not need as much water. But if the days are hot, and a wind is blowing, water evaporates very quickly and you may have to water your plant every day. You can, at this time, put a little extra water in the saucer and let the plant soak this up as needed.

In the winter, a heated house dries out the soil, and a plant may have to be watered often. To overcome dry, heated air, put a small tray filled with water under your plant, to add moisture to the air around it. But leave the plant in its saucer so that it won't absorb extra water. Dull days without sun mean less use of water by a plant, so beware of soggy soil.

Spring and fall are a mixture of both summer and winter, as they are sometimes hot, sometimes cold. Plants which have been slow growers during the winter will start to put out new shoots and leaves in the spring, and then the plant will need more water.

In any season, the old rule that says you should let the pot dry out before watering again is a killer. If you follow this rule and let the soil get hard and dry, then soak the plant, you'll cause problems.

Part of the roots will have dried up, and cannot take up a quick flood of water. In a few hours or a day, the plant may have recovered and the leaves are back up in their proper position. But then the edges of the leaves will start to turn brown and stay that way. Some of the branches which were supplied with water by the now-dried-up roots may wither and fall off.

If you have forgotten to water the plant, then give it just enough to moisten the soil. Wait for an hour, then give it more water. This way, the leaves will recover a bit and be ready for more water. The roots, too, will start to recover.

There is another old superstition that you cannot water a houseplant at night. Maybe this comes from the time when houses were not heated at night and very little in the daytime. But when plants are outside they get rain both day and night. In the tropics, quick storms come along at any time, even when the sun is shining. Some indoor plants may not want wet leaves at night. This is not a problem, though, because you are only putting water on the soil, not the plant. So, water your plants whenever you need to, both at a good time for you and for the plant.

To test for moisture, put your finger on the top of the soil. If it feels cool and damp, then it is wet enough. But if the soil feels dry, even when you wiggle your finger down about a half inch, then the plant needs water. A dry pot will feel very light, too.

It is best to water from the top. Let the water run through to the saucer below. Allow the plant to stand for five to ten minutes in the saucer full of water. The soil will absorb what it needs, as sometimes water just runs through without thoroughly moistening the soil. This happens when the soil is too dry. Then empty the saucer.

When you water from the top, you are also cleaning the soil of unused fertilizer. The clean water runs through, drains out, and is thrown away. Be careful, though, when watering from the top that you do not add so much water at once that you float off the top soil.

If you see bubbles on the top surface of the soil as you water it, then there are air pockets below. This is

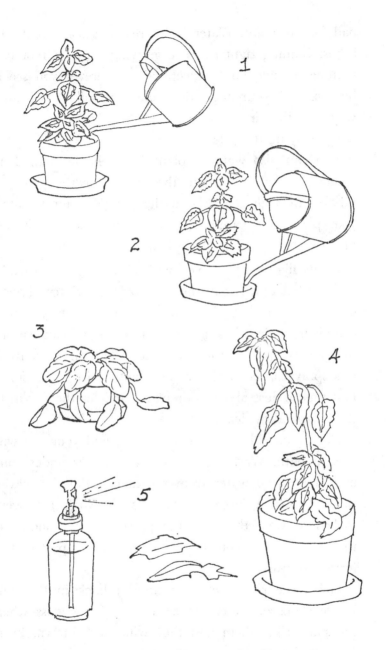

WATERING AND SPRAYING. 1. Top watering of plant. 2. Bottom watering of plant. 3. Overwatered African Violet. 4. Underwatered Coleus. 5. Spray bottled filled with clear water.

bad for the plant. Water is not reaching some roots. It is just running right by. The growing tip of a root has nothing to hold on to except air. Wherever you see a bubble, push your finger down into the soil. It will give way, and the air pocket will be filled. Add extra soil to completely fill the hole.

You can also water a plant from the bottom. This means pouring water into the saucer for the plant to take in through the hole in the pot. You must watch your plant very carefully, though, to be sure it is not underwatered nor left sitting in a saucer of water.

Plants like to be sprayed with clear water, especially on very hot days, or in the dry house in winter. Try to do this once a day. Use a well-washed, empty cleaning container which has a spray top, or fill an empty mouthwash spray bottle with water. The fine mist from this spray top is ideal for the plants. Direct the spray into the air just above your plant, and let the fog drift down around the leaves.

Dust, too, will settle on the leaves, and your pet will need a bath. Wash it off every two weeks under running, lukewarm water from the faucet. But first cover the soil with a piece of plastic so it won't get over-soaked or washed out in the process. Twist and turn the plant so that both underside and upper part of the leaves are washed.

Shake the plant before putting it back in the sun. Large drops of water act as a magnifying glass when the sun strikes them and they will cause brown, burn spots on the leaves.

Some furry leaves can be brushed off with a soft, broad watercolor brush.

YOUR OUTDOOR GARDEN

Outdoors, watering is even less of a routine affair. The amount of water you give the plants is based on the amount of rain that they have received. After one or more days of rain, wait until the top surface of the garden looks dry.

Always use a fine spray head on the watering hose or can. Never direct a heavy stream of water at the plants. You'll knock them down, or wash the dirt away from their roots.

During long, bright, hot days, water the garden early in the morning if you can. This will give the plants water to help them through the hot day ahead. The water will not evaporate right away, as it would in the heat of the day. The leaves will still be cool from the night air, and will not mind the cold water pouring over them. Be sure, if your plants grow very close together, that enough water is getting through the leaves and reaching the soil.

As you work with plants, you will find that each one has its own demands for water. One greedy plant will never seem to get enough water. Another will go a week before needing any. And a plant such as the cactus rarely needs water at all.

Now you might be wondering what to feed your pet, so next comes a description of a plant pet's diet.

Chapter 5

PLANTS HAVE TO EAT

Plants, in addition to needing light and water, need food. They are not fed like other pets, though, as they only need a little food once a week, and sometimes only every other week. A small five-ounce can or bottle of all-purpose plant food will seem to last forever. All you will use will be one-quarter to one teaspoon of powdered or liquid food in a quart of water. If you have just one plant, then you'll be using *one-eighth* of this amount in one-half cup of water. And you won't use the whole one-half cup, either!

The label directions on the proportion of *fertilizer* to water are based on a quart or a gallon of water. So you'll have to do some fast arithmetic to bring the quantity down to the amount your plant can use.

Look for a series of numbers on the front, side, or back label of the box or bottle of food. These will tell you the mixture of food in the container, and how strong it is.

Let's start with a balanced diet in which all the numbers are the same, such as 20-20-20.

The first number always represents *Nitrogen*. This is very important for growing healthy leaves. If your plant likes acid soil, this number should be equal or higher than the other two numbers.

The second number refers to *Phosphorus*. This is needed to develop roots and flowers.

The third number is for *Potash,* which is sometimes called *Potassium*. This is an all-around useful food. It helps the plant to absorb the other two foods, and also encourages flowering. A high third number prevents leaves from yellowing around the edges.

You will also see a number of other minerals and chemicals mentioned on the label. These will be in small quantities, and are known as *trace elements*. These work like vitamins to keep a plant growing.

If you have a very green-leaved plant from the jungle which is not a flowering type, use either the even formula, or one in which the first number is highest, for instance 30-10-10.

But for a flowering plant, like an African Violet, you would look for a formula with the second number highest, 5-8-7, for example. This type of formula is labeled African Violet Food. Any other fertilizer with a high middle number will do.

All the growing chemicals are mixed with a "bulking" powder or liquid to thin them out. If they were too concentrated, just a small error in measuring them out would be harmful to your plant. Its roots would be burned. So when you feed your plant, try using a bit less fertilizer than the manufacturer suggests. Also, add the fertilizer water only when the soil is moist. If the soil is dry, add a little clear water first, and let it soak down into the pot. This also will keep the roots from being burned, even by the right amount of food in the water.

Your pet will appreciate regular feedings. Pick a day that is best for you. Give your plant its fertilizer water each week on that day.

Another way of feeding your plant is the professional method, with every watering. Then you don't have to remember which day the plant will be hungry. But this doesn't mean that you will overfeed it. You just give it less food each watering, and by the end of the week it has received its full amount.

Find a clean quart-size plastic or glass bottle. Put a tiny pinch of fertilizer in the container and fill with water. You might use about one-eighth of a teaspoon. Put the top back on so the water will not evaporate. Then, every time you water, add about one-half teaspoon of this mixture to each cup of water.

If you have several plants, some green and some flowering, then you will have to make up two mixtures. One mixture should have a high first number for the green plants, and another, a high second number for the flowering ones. Label the containers so they won't get mixed up.

There are two other materials which are really not foods but are very necessary in keeping plants healthy.

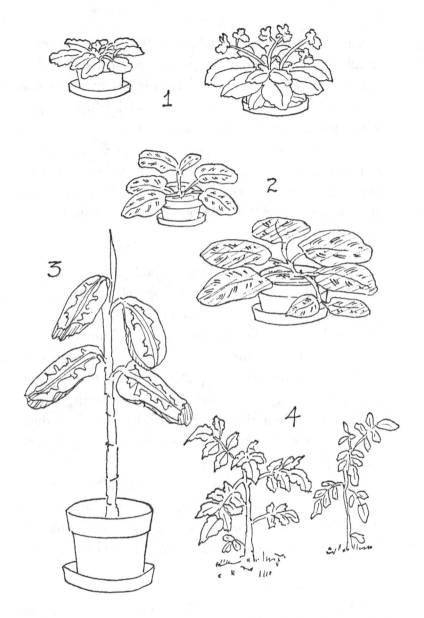

PLANTS NEED FOOD. 1. African Violet, *left*—unfed plant; *right*—
fed with high 2nd number food. 2. Prayer Plant, *left*, unfed
plant; *right*, fed high 1st number food for dark-green leaves.
3. Dieffenbachia—needs high 1st and 3rd number food for
brown-edged leaves. 4. Tomato—*left*, fed high 2nd and 3rd
number food for dark leaves and flowers; *right*, unfed plant.

One is *chelated iron,* which is sold as a powder in small amounts. Some types are rust-colored, others black. Buy either one. Iron is needed by acid-loving plants to keep their leaves green and healthy. If your plant starts to get yellow leaves, but the veins stay green, add chelated iron quickly. Add it directly to the soil in the amount the manufacturer suggests. Sprinkle the iron on top of the soil in the pot. Scratch it into the surface with a fork. Then water enough to moisten the surface.

The other material is lime, which prevents an acid soil. It is also important in building cell walls. The use of lime has been mentioned in the chapter on soils, but here is more detailed information. Add lime to your soil-less mixture in the form of ground, uncooked eggshells. Use a mortar and pestle to grind them up, or put them in a plastic bag and crush them with a rolling pin, or put them in the blender to reduce them to fine pieces. Add about a teaspoon to a cup of soil-less mix.

The ground eggshells also can be added to the top of the soil in a pot by sprinkling them over the surface. Turn the soil over a bit so the lime works into the top half-inch layer. Then water enough to moisten the top surface.

WORD OF WARNING: For about one day the soil will stink. But the smell goes away, and your plant will be grateful for the lime you've given it.

Outdoor garden feeding is usually planned well in advance of planting. The fertilizers, such as dried manure or a chemical formula, are turned into the soil when it is being prepared in the spring. See Chapter 3 for directions. Additional dry fertilizer is put on top of the soil once or twice during the summer. This is usually a 5-10-10 mixture.

Now that your plants are well-fed and growing, watch for any unusual and unexplained yellowing of the leaves. This may mean that bugs are trying to be well-fed by eating away at your plants. The next chapter will tell you what to look for in the way of pests.

Chapter 6

GETTING RID OF PESTS

There is always a certain amount of doctoring to do when you have a pet. Cats and dogs have fleas, get distemper, have to be wormed, need shots. Sometimes you can be the doctor, other times it's off to the veterinarian for you and the pet.

But *you* can take care of your plant's illnesses, or ask the advice of someone who is a good plant grower. Here are some helpful hints on the most common pests.

Yellowing, dropping leaves are a clue that something is attacking your pet. That is, if you have carefully watered and fed your plant, and kept it in the right light.

Plants do get bugs—not fleas—but their bugs are not interested in humans. They are strictly plant bugs.

Often the pests are on the plant when you buy it, so it is a good idea to look over the plant before you bring it home. Sometimes you cannot see any bugs on the plant. But the eggs are there and will hatch out once the plant is in your home. So, keep your new plant pet away from other plants for at least two weeks.

At other times, bugs just seem to blow in on the air, and settle on your well-cared-for plant. In August, when the air is hot and damp, *mealy bugs* suddenly appear on African Violets that never had a bug before. Or *scale* will show up on some other plant.

Mealy bugs are the easiest pests to see, and should be removed right away. Otherwise they take forever to get rid of. Look underneath all the leaves, and in the crack where a leaf stem joins the main stem. If you see a fluffy white spot which looks like a one-sixteenth to a one-eighth inch scrap of marshmallow, or a misplaced piece of perlite, you've found a mealy bug.

To remove this pest use a Q-tip or a toothpick wrapped with cotton or a piece of face tissue dipped in rubbing alcohol to lift off the mealy bug. Underneath that fluffy coat is a small, pinkish-tan bug with lots of legs. After you've cleaned off all the mealy bugs in sight, soak a piece of cotton or face tissue in the rubbing alcohol. Wipe off the backs and fronts of all the leaves, and the stems. This will kill any eggs or baby bugs.

Put the plant in a place away from all the other plants for two weeks. Check the backs of the leaves every day. After a week or two you may have to wipe the leaves again with alcohol. But chances are the mealy bugs are gone, and your plant is in the clear again.

Spider mites are the pests your plants may suffer from all through the year and especially in the winter. There are either red mites or two-spotted mites and they are so small that you cannot see them even with a regular magnifying glass. If the leaves of your plant are turning yellow and dropping off, you may have mites. The yellow and green will be sort of mottled.

Take a magnifying glass, and carefully go over the backs of all the leaves. You'll not be able to see the bugs, but if you see a fine white trail like a spider web, then you do have mites. With a 10-power loupe you would be able to see the small mites.

The best way to rid your plant of these pests is to use running water. Protect the soil surface with a piece of plastic wrap. Hold the plant upside down under a fully opened water faucet of lukewarm water. Wash the plant thoroughly. Dead leaves will fall off. Wash the under and upper sides of the leaves, letting the water bounce hard on the leaves. Repeat every two days. Mites do not like water. They thrive on dry leaves in a room that has very little humidity.

White flies are another troublesome pest. They are very small, but can be seen on the underside of leaves. If you tap a plant sharply, and see tiny white flakes fly upward, you know your plant pet has white flies. Seen under a magnifying glass they are absolutely white, like feathery moths, or fairy-tale creatures. However, they and their young suck juices from the leaves, which then turn yellow and fall off.

The way to cure your plant of white flies without using poison is to swish the whole plant in a deep bowl filled with lukewarm water to which you have added one-half to one teaspoon of liquid detergent. Protect the soil with a piece of plastic wrap, so that you can turn the pot over. Keep your fingers on the top of the soil so it won't fall out of the pot. Let the liquid dry on the leaves. Allow the plant to stand for a day, then wash off the leaves with clear water. Repeat the detergent bath.

The eggs of the white fly hatch out within two or three days. The tiny white bumps you see all over the backs of the leaves are the eggs. You may have to keep up the dipping and washing and drying for two weeks. Once the white fly pest is completely destroyed it will not return.

Scale is an indoor pest that is large enough to see without a magnifying glass. It is a bug which lurks on the underside of leaves and on stems. If you see sticky spots on the top of a leaf, turn over the leaf *above,* as a scale may be munching away. Since you never get just one scale, you'll soon find them all over the plant! Scale bugs are oval, flat and shiny, with a hard, light-brown shell. They are one-eighth to one-sixteenth of an inch long. Clinging flatly to the leaves and stems, they never seem to move.

The best way to remove these pests is to wipe the surface of the leaf with rubbing alcohol using a Q-tip or just a plain piece of cotton or face tissue. Remove all the scale on both sides of the leaves, and on the stems. Check every few days for the return of the pests. You might also wipe the leaves without scale, just in case.

These directions will take care of all the indoor plant

pests which can be treated with water and rubbing alcohol, and these are the ones you are most likely to find on your pet.

Sometimes you will see light-brown, quarter-inch-long, thin little bugs jumping around on top of the soil when you water a plant. These are more or less harmless *springtails*. The best way to get rid of them is to pour water into the top of the pot. Then tip the pot sideways and pour off water and springtails into the sink. Repeat with every watering, and the pests will soon be gone.

Snails are small outdoor plant pests, which can become indoor ones, if carried in the plant pots brought in from a greenhouse or plant store. They are about one-eighth to one-quarter of an inch across, with a hard brown circle of a shell. They move slowly up the stem and onto the leaves, munching as they go. If your plant's leaves look as if something had been nibbling at the edges, a snail has been there, and is still around somewhere. So start looking.

When you find the snail, or snails, remove it from the plant or pot and flush it down the sink. This is another reason for immediately repotting a plant in a soilless mixture when you bring it home.

Slugs are snails without the shells. These too may turn up, and treat them the same as snails.

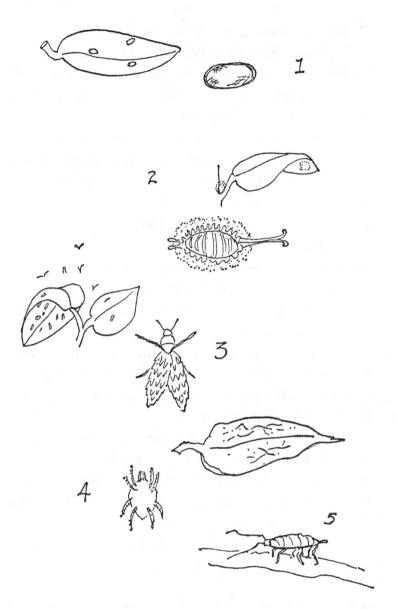

PLANT PESTS. 1. Scale—on leaf and enlarged view. 2. Mealy bug—on leaf and enlarged view. 3. White fly—flying around and on leaf and enlarged view. 4. Spider mite—white web on leaf and enlarged view. 5. Aphid—enlarged view on stem.

Aphids, or plant lice, are usually found only on out-door plants, particularly vegetables like lettuce and to-matoes and some flowering plants. These are small, soft-bodied bugs which sometimes have wings. They are pale green in color, but their corpses turn white. Usually rainstorms or hose watering takes care of these pests. If not, pour soapy or mild-detergent water over the plants, and let the solution dry on them. If there is no rain, in a couple of days hose off the plants with clear water. Next day use soapy water again.

You may have to repeat this process several times. In the house, once you have gotten rid of a particular pest your plant is fairly safe. Outdoors, there is always the chance that pests will move over from all the other plants for miles around into your garden.

Aphids *can* appear on indoor plants as well. Sometimes when plants are put outside during the summer, they attract the pests. When they are brought indoors in the fall, the pests go along.

And, if you plant tomato, lettuce, or carrot seeds indoors, the chances are that you will raise a crop of aphids, as well as white flies. Some seeds have not been treated for pests at the seed house, so mixed in with them are the unseen eggs. These hatch, along with the plant seeds, and both grow up together. Again, use soapy water to get rid of the bugs.

Early repotting of new plants cuts down on the chance of bringing pests into the house from the plant store, and using your own soil mixture instead of out-side soil cuts down the chance of pests attacking your plants still further. Outside, soil and plants and bugs are pretty well ecologically balanced. Bugs in the soil and ones that go from soil to plant, or from leaf to leaf, have natural enemies. Ladybugs go from plant to plant cleaning up the aphids. Birds help to clean up the soil and plants too. And in the large commercial gardens, greenhouses, and farms, bug sprays are used on plants and soil.

But, inside your house there are none of these natural enemies and you will want to avoid using chemicals and poisonous sprays. So, by following these directions you can concentrate on keeping your plants free of pests. It may take a little more work and time follow-ing these methods, but it is well worth the trouble. Your plants will be healthier for that extra care you give them.

So, now that the plant is growing well in all direc-tions, it may be looking too tall or shaggy. It's probably time to trim it back to houseplant size.

Chapter 7

GIVING YOUR PLANT
A HAIRCUT

All growing things get bigger. A kitten becomes a cat, and a puppy becomes a dog. Both cat and dog are much larger than they were when they were young. Plants get larger too. What began as a small plant in a small pot, becomes a bigger plant to put in a bigger pot. And a still bigger pot will be needed as the plant grows even larger.

But the size of a plant can be controlled. The results will be even better than just a haircut for a dog, though at first it seems to be the same process. A dog's hair will grow out again in the same way, but trimming a plant changes its whole shape.

When a plant starts to grow tall and leggy, with one long center stem instead of a short and branching center growth, cut it back. No, you won't be harming it, and you won't kill it. A few plants cannot be cut back, but those are described later on.

The cutting back or trimming varies with each plant. Some plants are allowed to grow upward until there are six or eight leaves on the stem, or one or two side branches. When you are starting a plant from a seed, you can trim it at the four-leaf stage.

Once you have bought a plant and it is well-settled

in its new home, you can start trimming it with scissors or a small, sharp knife. This will keep it short, force branches and new leaves to grow, and turn it into a bushy shape.

If the leaves grow in pairs, that is, opposite each other on the stem, cut off the top two leaves to just one-quarter of an inch above the next two leaves. If the leaves are single, alternating up the stem, then cut back to one-quarter inch above the third leaf.

This cutting stops the plant stem from growing upward, and forces it to put out side shoots. Sometimes shoots also will be forced out along the lower part of the stem. In most cases, two new shoots or stems will start to grow, one on each side of the main stem. They will pop out from the angle where the two topmost leaves join the stem. There is a little growing bud here, so never cut the main stem too close to this spot.

When these two new stems have several leaves, again cut off their two top leaves. Two new shoots will start to grow. If other branches have grown farther down the stem, cut these back too.

In this way, your plant will develop many new branches, and begin to form a sturdy bush. The center stem will also get thicker at the base, and be better able to hold the plant upright. It also helps a plant to be trimmed after it has been transplanted. A smaller plant with less leaves gives the roots a chance to recover. They do not have to supply a large plant with food and water.

Sometimes by putting a plant in a Japanese pot, you

can give it a whole new look. It will look like a little tree.

Measurements given are approximate. Some plants need to have longer stems cut off, or the leaves are closer together, or farther apart. You will learn to judge where and how much to trim off a plant. You will also hear some people refer to "pinching" a plant. This is just cutting off the top growing tip of a plant, usually the tiny, beginning leaves.

If you want to make a plant really bushy and small, trim it back to just the first four leaves. Then it will start to branch from this level.

A plant which has many branches may need another type of trimming. It may have too crowded a look. Carefully examine the plant. Turn it around so you can get an all-around view. Then trim away some of the branches, and some of the tips, so that the plant has an open look.

WHEN NOT TO TRIM

Plants which do not have a real center stem, like African Violets, cannot be trimmed. Their leaves really come up from a center area, just under the top surface of the soil. Leaves are added only in a circle as the plant grows upward. If the top center leaves are cut away, the plant will stop growing completely. African Violets often develop what looks like a stem—called a neck—which should be under the soil line. A plant

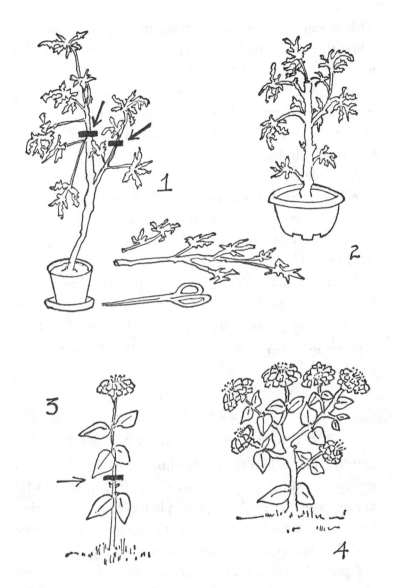

TRIMMING PLANTS—INDOORS AND OUTDOORS. 1. Plant trimmed back. Arrows show cuts. 2. New branches from the top and along the stem. Plant repotted in a Japanese pot to make it look special. 3. Zinnia growing straight up, one flower only. 4. Zinnia has branched after being cut back.

with a long neck needs repotting to bury it in the soil. Then the rosette of leaves will be on the surface of the soil again.

Another nontrimming plant is a Palm tree, which grows straight up, with a longer center stem and a tuft of leaves called fronds at the top. Cut off this top and the plant will die.

Also, plants without even a center neck, whose separate leaves come up from the soil, cannot be trimmed. Cut back the leaf and it stays cut back. Nothing new develops. These are plants like the Spider Plant, and the Prayer Plant.

To groom these plants, take off any dead leaves, yellow leaves, dead branches. Cut off the brown ends on the leaves of Spider Plants. This should be done as a general practice, even if you are not trimming the plant.

YOUR OUTDOOR GARDEN

Outdoor plants also need a trimming to force them into sturdy growth. This job is often done by rabbits, who nip away at the tender tops of plants. They are looking for food, but their action helps the plant to grow more branches. So pretend you are a rabbit and nip away.

Again, the rules that are given for indoor plants are also good for outdoor plants. A plant such as the Zinnia branches out nicely when cut back. Tall, unbranched plants like corn, or plants with leaves coming out of the ground without stems like lettuce and carrots, cannot be cut back.

While you are trimming the plants, do a little grooming in your garden. Take off the dead leaves and flowers so that new flowers will develop. Do not remove tomato flowers, as you want these to develop into fruit.

Pull out the weeds in your garden. Hoe the soil between the plants so that water will soak down into the soil, and not run off a hard surface. A broken-up surface also keeps the underground water from evaporating too quickly.

Now that you have learned where and how to trim a plant, use the trimmings to start new plants. Read the next chapter for information on how one plant can turn into many plants.

Chapter 8

STARTING YOUR OWN
PLANT FACTORY

Making new plants from the ones you have is fun and
very easy. In this way your own collection will get
larger and you'll have plants to give away to friends.
Also, if anything happens to the original plant, you will
have a new one to take its place. Here are some of the
ways to grow new plants from your original one.

METHOD ONE: STEM CUTTINGS

This is one of the easiest and quickest ways to grow
new plants. You can use the trimmings which you cut
from your plant as described in the last chapter. But
trim off a length of stem which has at least six leaves.
This way you'll be both trimming your plant and making a new plant with the piece cut off.

First, gather together the following: a pair of small,
sharp scissors, a small plastic pot or plastic food container (the size depends on how many cuttings you are
going to make), enough vermiculite to fill the container, a grease pencil or crayon to mark the pot, and a
root-growing powder, such as Rootone or Hormodin.
These powders which help to prevent the stem from
rotting in the damp vermiculite or soil make it possible

to get roots on almost any cutting. They are sold in plant and variety stores in small containers of $\frac{1}{4}$ ounce to 2 ounces. You will only need a small amount for each cutting. Lastly, have ready a small brush to apply the powder to the bottom of the plant stem, a plastic bag, a twister seal, and your plant pet. Now you're ready to begin.

If you are using a food container, punch a hole in the bottom with a hot nail. This is for drainage in case you put too much water in the pot. Pour in the vermiculite. Add a little water, and stir it into the vermiculite. If the mixture is too dry, add more water but, the vermiculite should be just damp, not soaking wet, or your cutting will rot. If it is too wet, let the vermiculite dry out a bit.

With the end of a pencil, make a hole in the center of the vermiculite. If you are planting several cuttings, then scatter the holes around the pot. Make as many holes as you have cuttings. They can be close together.

The next step is to make your cutting. If the leaves are opposite each other, you will want the cutting to have six to eight pairs of leaves. If the leaves alternate up the stem, then six leaves will do. These numbers are only approximate, as a great deal depends on the size of the leaves, and how far apart they are along the stem.

Always hold the cutting by a *leaf,* never by the stem. The plant or cutting can always grow another leaf, but a pinched stem can never be replaced, and the plant will wither and die. All the plant's sap goes up the stem like blood moves through our arteries.

Cut the stem between leaves. Then snip off the lowest leaf or two on the cutting, almost to the stem. The new roots will grow out of the places where the leaves were. Dust the lower stem, including the two leaf-joining areas, with root-growing powder, using the small brush. Shake off the extra powder.

Carefully put the stem into the hole in the vermiculite. Close up the hole around the stem by pushing the vermiculite against it. Be sure the vermiculite touches the stem all the way down to the bottom.

Mark the pot with the plant's name.

Place the pot and cutting inside the plastic bag. Almost close the top of the bag. Then, with the pot resting on a flat surface, blow into the narrowed top of the bag to fill it with air. Tie the top with a twister seal. This extra *carbon dioxide* will help the cutting grow, and keep the sides and top of the bag away from the cutting.

Place the pot and bag in a bright place, but *not* in the sun. Sun shining through the plastic bag will cook the cutting. You will not need to water the pot, as the plastic bag will keep the moisture in. Do not open the bag unless a lot of water forms on the inside surface. Then you will know that the vermiculite is too wet. If this happens, open the bag for a day to dry things out, otherwise your cutting will rot. Then retie the bag.

After two weeks, open the bag. Hold the plant by a lower leaf and give it a slight tug. If the cutting does

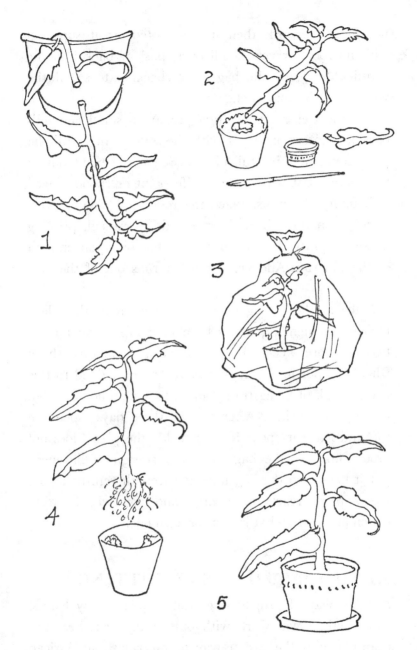

METHOD ONE: Stem Cutting. 1. Tip cut from plant for propagation. 2. Cutting with one leaf snipped off has been brushed with root-growing powder and is being put into vermiculite. 3. Placed in plastic bag. 4. Cutting with roots. 5. Planted in soil-less mix.

not move upward, then it has rooted. If it slips out with no roots or very small ones, push it back into the vermiculite. Retie the bag after checking to see if the vermiculite is moist enough.

For the well-rooted cutting prepare a small one-and-one-half- to two-inch pot with the soil-less mix. Fill the pot about one-third full of soil. Scoop the plant out of the rooting pot with a dull knife point or spoon placed well under the roots. Place the roots and clinging vermiculite on the soil in the pot. Add more soil, pressing it down lightly. Fill the pot to within one-quarter inch of the top rim. Add water until it runs out of the bottom hole.

Place a plastic bag over the pot to help the plant recover. Remember, it has been in damp warm air for two or more weeks. It will suffer a temporary shock when it is put in the dry air of the room. Added to this is the shock of being transplanted to a new home. Close the top of the bag. After two or three days, open the top and leave it open. If after a day the plant does not droop, take off the bag. At the first sign of limpness, put it back into the bag until its strength returns again. Every plant reacts differently, and you will have to watch and learn what is best for each one.

METHOD TWO: LEAF CUTTINGS

Another way of propagating from a plant is by leaves. This method will work with only a few varieties. For example, it is the easiest way to propagate an African Violet plant.

You will need a three-inch pot, damp vermiculite, a pencil, a clean, sharp knife, root powder, a plastic bag, and a twister seal. Then, follow these simple directions.

First, fill the three-inch pot with damp vermiculite. Make a hole in the middle with the pencil. Cut off a stem and leaf from the second row of leaves. An outer, older leaf sometimes takes too long to root. Leave about one and one-half inches of stem attached to the leaf. Dip the end in rooting powder. Put it down into the hole until the top surface of the vermiculite is level with the bottom of the leaf where it joins the stem. Push the vermiculite close to the stem. You can put several leaves in the same pot.

Cover the pot with a small plastic bag, and tie at the top. Put it in a light, but not sunny spot.

New plants can take up to two months to appear, so do not be discouraged. You will see tiny leaves forming at the surface of the vermiculite, just at the center rib of the leaf where it joins the stem. Several plants may develop. When leaves and roots are well along, cut away from the mother leaf and put each plant in a very small separate pot.

Put each pot inside a plastic bag, until the plants are settled in their new home. Loosen the bag after a week, and take it off completely at the end of two weeks.

METHOD THREE: PLANTLETS

This method also involves special plants. Both the Spider Plant and the Strawberry Geranium share this

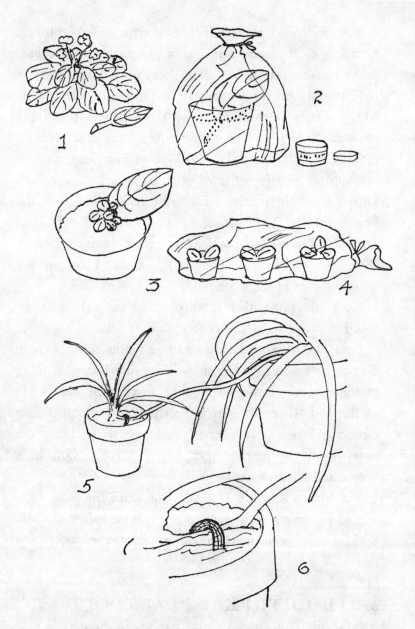

METHOD TWO: Leaf Cuttings. 1. African Violet plant. 2. Leaf in damp vermiculite. Pot inside plastic bag. 3. New plants at end of leaf. 4. New plants in their own pots inside plastic bag. METHOD THREE: Plantlets. 5. Plantlet of Spider Plant pinned down in pot. 6. Closeup of runner and hairpin.

method. Both grow plantlets at the end of a long runner, and do not have a center stem.

Place a small pot filled with soil mixture beside the original pot. Place the plantlet in the center of the pot while it is *still attached to the mother plant by its runner*. Scratch a little hole in the center, so some of the soil is heaped up around the base of the plantlet. Hold the plantlet in position with a hairpin placed over the runner, then pushed down into the soil. Water, and wait for the new roots to grow. Then cut the runner with scissors. If you want the mother plant pot to get full of plants, pin the plantlets into the soil around the main plant.

METHOD FOUR: AIR-LAYERING

Using this method, you can grow a new plant without using a pot. And, the cutting will not be removed from the plant until the roots are formed.

Air-layering can only be used with certain plants. These are mostly single stem or woody, shrubby plants with thick stems.

You will need a clean, sharp knife. Also have ready wet vermiculite, or wet sphagnum moss (when using moss, be sure it is fresh sphagnum moss, not ground-up milled sphagnum), a piece of plastic food-wrap, two twister seals or sticky tape, root-growing powder, and a small brush. Be sure all your supplies are close at hand, as this can be a rather delicate operation.

Near the top bunch of leaves, cut a "V"-shaped slit

in the stem, one to two inches long and one-eighth to one-quarter inch deep, using a sharp knife. This is usually done when a plant has grown very tall with only a bunch of leaves at the top of a long, bare, single stem or bare branches. The slit is made lengthwise along the stem. Now make two more slits around the stem at the same level. You will end up with three cuts around the stem at an even distance apart.

Using the small brush, dust the cuts with root-growing powder. Then, wrap the plastic wrap around the stem, several times, just below the bottom of the cuts. Keep it tight for a one-inch depth around the stem. The rest of the wrap should be loose enough to form a bag. The wrap will reach above the cuts, with room to spare, as it is going to be filled with sphagnum moss or vermiculite.

Fill the wrap with moist vermiculite or sphagnum moss, supporting it with one hand as you do so. Work some of the material into the slits. The roots will grow out of the slits into this moist material. Make a nice big lump of it all around the stem, about two and one-half inches thick. It will reach one inch above the top of the slits. Close the top with twister seals, or sticky tape. Now you have a plastic bandage filled with moist growing material.

Depending on the plant, the roots will show through the packing material in four to six weeks. Check the water in the material every two weeks by untying the top fastening and sticking a finger down into the packing. If it is dry, carefully add a little water until it is moist, then refasten.

64

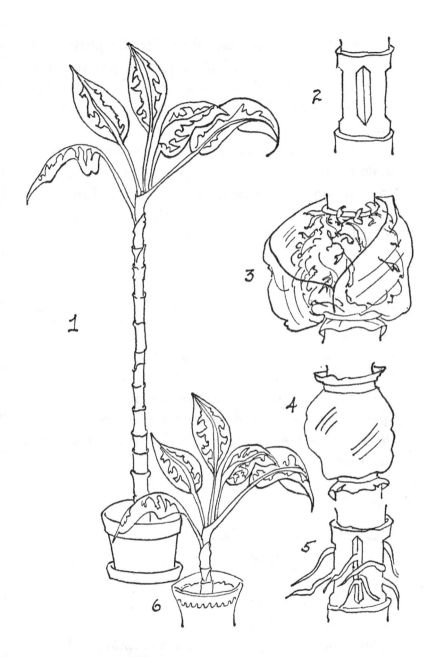

METHOD FOUR: Air-layering. 1. A long-stemmed Dieffenbachia.
2. "V"-shaped slits in stem. 3. Sphagnum moss in place. 4. Plastic
"bag" tied around sphagnum. 5. Roots growing out of cuts.
6. Top of plant growing in new pot.

When the roots are showing under the plastic, cut the stem just *below* the ball of packing material. Remove the plastic, and plant top and roots in a pot full of soil-less mix. You can leave the packing material around the roots.

The original plant may grow up again from the roots, so do not take it out of its pot. Just cut the stem back if there are no branches or leaves on the plant. Leave five inches sticking up from the top of the soil level. A good plant for air-layering is a Dieffenbachia.

METHOD FIVE: SECTIONING

When a plant's leaves come up from the soil with no center stem, like a Prayer Plant, or a Spider Plant, there is still a fifth method of propagating new plants. Take the plant out of the pot. Gently pull sections apart and repot these in separate pots. Be sure to soak the plant well before taking it out of the pot. Also water well after repotting.

METHOD SIX: SEEDS

This method is used to start annual and perennial plants outdoors. You can save the seeds from year to year as the seed pods are formed on your plants, or you can buy new seed at the store.

You can plant seeds outdoors in the spring and early summer. (See Chapter 3 for directions.) Or you can

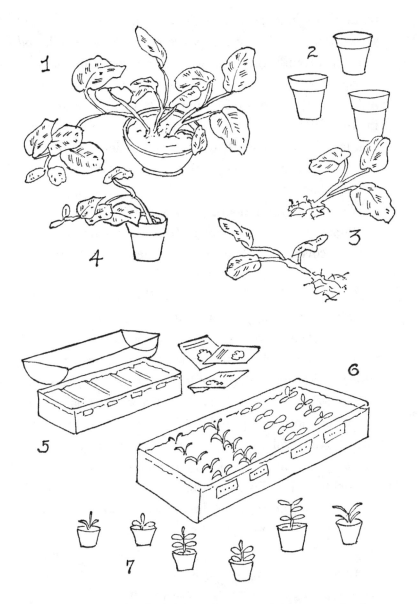

METHOD FIVE: Sectioning. 1. Pot containing several plants.
2. Small pots ready for the new planting. 3. Two sections pulled
apart. 4. One section in its new small pot. METHOD SIX: Seeds.
5. Covered box filled with vermiculite, packets of seeds. 6. Seedlings just coming up. 7. Some seedlings transplanted to pots.

plant them indoors at any time of the year. Seeds will sprout indoors whenever they are put into moist soil, and the air around them is warm. So you can plant a marigold seed indoors in November, and have flowers indoors in January or February. Or plant tomato seeds in the fall for winter tomatoes inside. Just put the plants on a sunny south window, or under a fluorescent lamp, which is especially good, as the plants never get a dull, sunless day.

Planting seeds indoors is easy. Use a clear plastic container with a clear cover. If the container does not have a cover, stretch a piece of clear food-wrap over the top after the seeds are planted.

Put two inches of vermiculite, slightly moist, in the container. Indoors, you will not have room for a lot of plants. Put only five or six seeds on top of the vermiculite. Space them far apart to make transplanting easier. Add three extra seeds in case all the seeds do not come up. Mark the names on a stick-on label, and put it on the box. Sprinkle *milled sphagnum moss* over them. This will cover the seeds as well as prevent *damp-off*. Damp-off is a *fungus* which causes seedlings indoors to just go limp and die.

Put the cover over the box. Do not take it off until the seedlings are ready to be transplanted into separate pots. Put the box in moderate light, not in the sun, but in an area just away from the window. Or put it under fluorescent light, not incandescent, as that is too hot.

At any time from a week to two weeks after planting, the first two leaves will show above the soil. Wait until two more leaves appear before transplanting. Then, fill small, two-inch pots with soil-less mix. Fill the pot almost to the top. Make a hole in the middle of the soil to hold the seedling. Hold the plant by the lowest leaf. Loosen the roots from the soil with the point of a dull knife. The plant will come up out of the vermiculite with some of the material still clinging to the roots. Quickly slip it into the hole. Press the soil firmly around the roots and stem.

Water the plant and put it inside a plastic bag. Continue to transplant the rest of the seedlings. Also put them into the plastic bag. Close the bag for a day or two until the plants recover. You may lose one or two. Open the bag a little. During the next few days, gradually open the bag wider, until you can take the bag off completely.

All these basic methods of propagating plants will give you lots of new plants to experiment with. You can use your cuttings in your new hanging basket (see pp. 21–23) to make a full, attractive plant. Just bunch several new small plants of one kind in the pot. The number of plants you'll use depends on their size, how quickly they will grow, and the size of the pot. If you have a four-inch pot, start with four or five plants, and space them around the edge, with one in the middle.

Or, use your cuttings to try out some or all of the projects described in the next chapter.

Chapter 9

PLANT PROJECTS TO TRY

Now that you've become a good grower of healthy plants, you can try new plants, or train your pets into new shapes. Try giving them a new, protected home of their own called a *terrarium*. Or grow an indoor tropical orchard from seeds. Or create a medieval herb garden either indoors or outdoors.

TRAINING PLANTS

The best plants for training into small tree shapes always have woody stems, branches, and small leaves. Like all pets, the younger you start training, the easier it will be. The more you train the plant into its new shape, the better it will behave as it continues to grow larger.

Training a plant is a little more than giving it a haircut. It includes bending branches into new and more interesting positions. The branches then have to be held there until they are growing naturally in their new direction. Hold the branches in place with a piece of soft string. Tie the string loosely around a branch. Pull down on the string until the branch is halfway to its final position. Then attach the end of the string to the side of the pot with sticky tape. After a month, pull the branch down to its final position and hold the string in place against the side of the pot. After two months cut the string away. The branch's new position will be permanent.

Sometimes when you repot a plant, you can angle the stem at a new slanting angle. Then train the branches to match. This gives a plant a whole new look.

Try out these suggestions on tropical fruit trees described on pages 78–79.

TRAINING VINES

On a Wire   Train vines such as a Purple Velvet Plant, Swedish Ivy, or Wandering Jew to grow in a diamond-shaped area. You'll need a wire coat hanger, pliers, two flat, half-inch-wide sticks of wood, fifteen inches of fine wire, and a five-inch clay pot (for this purpose a plastic pot is too light).

First, straighten out the coat hanger. Hold the wire at the hook side. Place the other hand in the middle of the opposite side. Holding the hanger in a horizontal position, pull the two hands apart until you have a fat, diamond shape.

Next, uncurl the hook with your pliers. This wire length and the twisted area up to the bottom of the diamond shape will be pushed into the soil in the pot. You might leave the very end of the hook unstraightened, as this will help to anchor the wire in the soil.

Finally, place two short flat sticks of wood, one-half inch wide, on each side of the straightened "hook" wire, holding them tightly in place with a wrapping of fine wire. This also will brace the wire in place.

Now put the stick-covered wire end into the center of a five-inch clay pot, and fill it halfway up with soil. Place two small plants on each side of the pot, near the base of the diamond. Spread out roots, and fill the pot with soil, leaving one-half inch at the top unfilled. Firm soil around the plants and the wire.

Each plant will be trained to grow up its own side of the diamond wire. Twist the ends of the plants around the wire, attaching them with twistems or very soft green cord. Do not squeeze the stems when tying them to the wire.

As the plants grow, tie the ends. Trim any extra pieces of plant that shoot out from the center design. Keep training and clipping until you have a thick outlined diamond shape.

On a Pole Make a small pole of woven wire using either hardware-cloth, or woven wire. Fill it with damp sphagnum moss. Plant a vine at the top. A Purple Velvet Plant would look great with its ends hanging over the length of the pole. Or, put several Strawberry Geraniums through the holes, and in the top opening. They will grow, and cover the wire. Keep pinning down the new runners with hairpins.

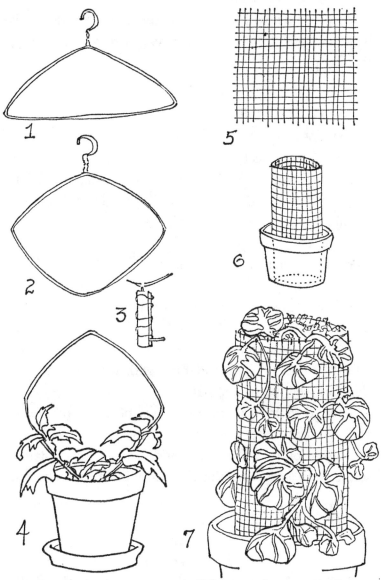

TRAINING VINES ON A WIRE. 1. Wire coat hanger. 2. Hanger pulled out into a diamond shape. 3. Wood sticks held by wire to the straightened hook. 4. Wire in pot with two Purple Velvet Plants tied to each side. ON A POLE. 5. Piece of woven wire 11 inches square. 6. Wire made into tube and put into a four-inch pot. 7. Tube filled with damp sphagnum moss, and planted with Strawberry Geraniums.

Your plants will look quite different, growing this way, and will be very decorative. These are nice ways to grow plants for gifts.

TERRARIUMS FOR SINGLE PLANTS

Another fun project is to grow plants in a covered glass jar. This makes a good home for plants that need lots of humidity in the air. Also, if you have "walking around" pets they cannot reach your plant pet, knock it over, or chew it up. A small Red-Nerved, or Dwarf-Nerved Fittonia, a Prayer Plant, or an African Violet are good choices.

You can use a large, straight-sided peanut butter or pickle jar. Scrub out all bits of food. Rinse out the jar with clear hot water to which a little chlorine has been added. Rinse out a second time with clear water. Dry the glass well, inside and out.

Then, dribble in a half-inch layer of *damp* perlite. If you use dry perlite, a fine white dust will settle all over the inside of your jar. Next add two inches of damp, soil-less mix, choosing the right formula to match your plant.

Make a hole in the center, large enough to hold the roots of the plant. It is best to use a long-handled spoon or stick to do this. Take the plant out of its pot, and clean off some of the soil from the roots. Hold the plant gently between two upright sticks, and guide it into the jar and down into the hole. Add enough damp soil to cover the roots. Brush off the plant leaves and the sides of the jar, removing all small bits of soil. Do not add any more water.

Cover the top of the jar with clear food-wrap and hold it in place with a rubber band. Now you have a completely sealed world. Put it on a north window sill, or away from direct sunlight at an east or west window. The water in the soil will evaporate into the air in the jar. It will turn back into water, and run down the sides of the jar into the soil. The plant will make its own carbon monoxide and oxygen. It will never need to be fertilized. The plant will grow slowly and will rarely need attention.

TERRARIUM LANDSCAPES

A larger closed-in scene can be made in a small aquarium filled part way with soil-less mix. You may have an old tank, or a friend who used to raise fish may give you one. It's called an aquarium when it has water (aqua) and fish in it, and a terrarium when it contains soil (terra) and plants. In either case it is still the same rectangular, glass container. Put in a few plants which like humid air, and some rocks and soil. Make a pretend pond, and a small hill, and you have made your own piece of world.

Here's how it's done. First, clean the aquarium, following the directions for cleaning a glass jar in the last section.

Next, cover the bottom of the rectangular container with one-half inch of perlite as you did with the small jar. If you want a pond in your garden, this is the time to decide where to put it. Leave an area covered only by perlite. Do not use soil here.

Now add a 1-1-1 mixture of peat moss, vermiculite, and perlite. Build it up to a higher level at the back of the terrarium. Leave other areas low and flat. The plants will stay in their pots, so the soil should be deep enough to hold the pots. By leaving the plant in the pot you will not disturb its roots.

Put plants and pots on top of the soil first to see where they will look best. Low plants should be in front, higher ones in back. The next step is to dig holes and sink the pots into the soil, and hide the top of the pot with a thin layer of soil. You can take a pot and plant out of the base soil and move it to another place, and no harm has been done to the plant. If it grows too big, out comes the plant and pot. Its roots have not spread into the roots of another plant, so the rest of the scene is not spoiled.

Add a few rocks to your scene. Sometimes, you can make a small cliff with two or three rocks and hide a pot behind them, with the plant showing over the top of the rocks. Add pebbles to cover the surface of the pool, or leave it plain perlite.

Always remember that the plants will grow larger, so leave space between them. At first planting, your scene should look bare, and soil should be showing between the plants. You want the effect of a hillside scene, not an overcrowded jungle that needs thinning. Give the

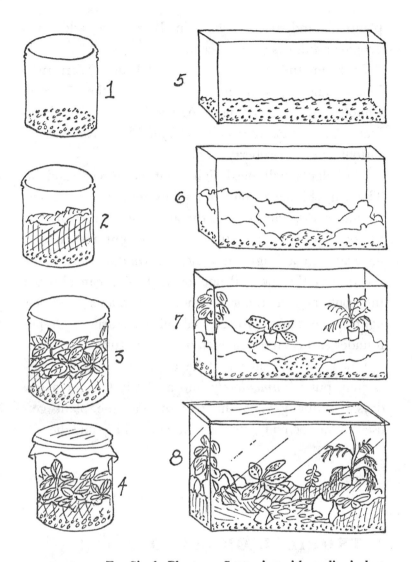

TERRARIUMS: For Single Plants. 1. Large jar with perlite in bottom. 2. Soil-less mix added. 3. Small *Fittonia minor* added. 4. Clear plastic tied over top. TERRARIUM LANDSCAPES. 5. Perlite covers bottom of "aquarium." 6. Soil-less mix formed into mountains, pond in center. 7. Plants in pots on top of mix. 8. Pots sunk into mix, rocks around pot in left corner. Rocks in front of pond. Pebbles covering pond area. Glass or plastic over top of terrarium.

plants air and space to grow in. If you like, add small people or animals to your scene.

Look in the store for plants labeled "Terrarium Plants" and try some new ones. Among the plants in Chapter 10, you can use: African Violet, Aluminum Plant, Coleus, Palm (small), Prayer Plant, Red-Nerved Fittonia, and Strawberry Geranium.

The plants will need light, but no direct sunlight. The sun, shining through the glass into the closed terrarium world, will heat up the air. The plants will start to cook, go limp, and turn black. So put the covered terrarium in a bright area near a window, but where the rays of the sun will not touch it. You can also put the container in a north window, as plants need less light in the damp, protected air of a terrarium. Or put it under two twenty-four-inch fluorescent tubes.

When you do have to take a plant out of the terrarium, put it *immediately* into a plastic bag for a few days. Gradually open the bag so that the plant gets used to the room air, otherwise it will go limp and die.

A TROPICAL ORCHARD

There are other special gardens you can grow indoors. What about a tropical fruit tree garden? You can never get any fruit, but you'll have nice small trees which you can keep cut back. It is fun to show off your orange, lemon, grapefruit, or avocado tree which you grew from seeds. In some areas which sell fruits and vegetables from the Caribbean Islands you can get tamarind fruit and grow a delicate, small-leaved tamarind tree from the seeds. Plant the seeds in vermiculite and cover with milled sphagnum moss. See the directions in Chapter 8, under Method Six.

An avocado seed is large, two to three inches long, so start in a four-inch pot. Fill the pot half full of 2-1-1 mix of peat moss, vermiculite, and perlite. Put the seed in the center of the pot with the pointed end up. Fill the rest of the pot with soil-less mix, pressing the soil down lightly around the seed, and leaving about three-fourths of an inch of seed showing above the soil. Water well and put on the sunny window sill. There is no exact length of time for sprouting, so just wait until the stem starts to show. When the stem is about ten inches tall, and has several leaves, cut it back to the first set of leaves. This will force it to branch.

Keep all the tropical trees cut back, and train them, following the directions in the first part of this chapter.

AN INDOOR HERB GARDEN

An herb garden indoors in the winter is a surprise to everyone. Pick out small herbs that grow well indoors. Herbs such as dill and caraway are too tall.

There are two ways to start your sweet-smelling garden. Buy seeds or buy plants. You can order plants by

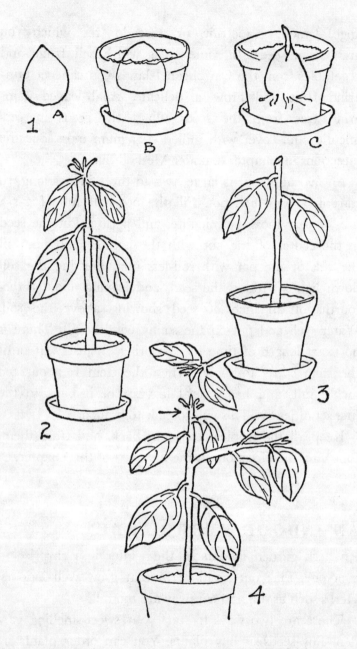

AVOCADO TREE. 1. A, Avocado pit; B, in a pot of soil-less mix; and C, the first sprout and roots. 2. Plant with two sets of leaves. 3. Plant cut back to first set of leaves. 4. First branch growing out above cut. Arrow shows where next cut will be made.

mail from special herb greenhouses (see p. 150). If you do this, order when the weather is warm. Most greenhouses will not ship in the winter, as the plants would freeze. Or you can buy seeds. Check a seed catalog under the list of "Herbs."

Plant basil, thyme, lavender *dentata,* rosemary, sage, pineapple sage, winter savory, marjoram. These are all warm Mediterranean herbs which are used to growing all year round in a warm place. In places where the winters are cold and summers are warm, these herbs are grown outdoors during the warm months, but they will die back in the winter time. Plants that die back for a time are called *dormant.* If the winter is not too cold, they may come up again in the spring.

In such a climate you can dig up the outdoor herbs in August, put them in a pot, and bring them indoors to a sunny window. In this way they will not get any frost, which would put them to sleep. Indoors in the warmth they stay awake all winter.

You can put several herb plants in a large plastic bowl with a line of pebbles between each plant. Or you can grow plants in five separate, triangle-shaped containers of a plastic Lazy Susan. These were originally made to hold dried beans and rice, and other dried things on a kitchen counter. Fill the containers with soil-less mix, and add plants. Put the sections and round bottom base in a sunny window, or under a fluorescent light on the kitchen counter.

Put a sage plant into a hanging pot. It will trail over the sides. Its clean, spicy smell will fill the room

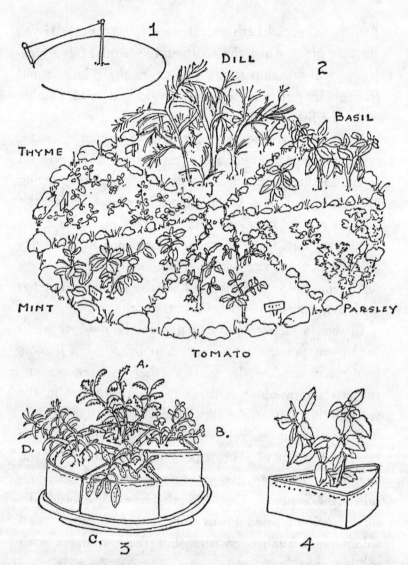

OUTDOOR HERB GARDEN. 1. Making the circle with two sticks and string. 2. Stones separate the planted sections. INDOOR HERB GARDEN. 3. Lazy Susan sections filled with soil-less mix and plants. A. Lavender *dentata*; B. Marjoram; C. Sage; D. Rosemary. 4. Basil in wedge container.

every time you touch it. The leaves can be used in cooking, either fresh or dried.

AN OUTDOOR HERB GARDEN

Medieval herb gardens were planted in raised beds of earth held in place by low stone walls. Usually these were in a pattern of small squares, or a wheel with spokes. You can make a small garden outside in late spring. Draw a circle with two sticks and a length of string. Mark out the spokes of a wheel with small stones. Edge the circle with small stones. Put your herb plants in position, placing one type of herb in each triangular bed. Instead of plants you can use seeds. Follow the directions for outdoor growing in Chapter 3.

As your collection of plants grows larger, you'll think of many things to do with them.

But first let's take a good look at some fun plants. They are arranged in alphabetical order with the best choices for indoor plants first and good outdoor plant choices next. Under the picture of each plant is a short description. Then follows a list of information about light, soil, water, food, bugs, trimming, and how to start new plants. The first plant on the list is one that can bloom almost all the time!

Chapter 10

PLANTS TO CHOOSE FROM
Pictures and Care Guide

INDOOR PLANTS

AFRICAN VIOLET
Saintpaulia

For lots of flowers on a small, low plant the best buy is an African Violet. The leaves spread out flat on long leaf stems in a circle wider than the top of the pot. The flower clusters stand up in the center. There are many varieties, with flowers either single or double, in pink, red, white, or blue. Look for 'Lisa' in the Ballet series, or any of the named violets in the Rhapsodie series. These plants are trademarked and are good for beginners, as they bloom well and are not too fussy about perfect care.

Light   Put the plant in a south, west, or east window, or under fluorescent lights. It needs good light to grow and bloom. In the summertime too much hot sun in a south window may turn the leaves pale green. Put the plant on a table a foot or so from the window.

Soil   The soil should be a rich mixture, but not as much peat moss as you will use with some of the jungle plants. Use a formula of 2-2-1 of peat moss, vermiculite, and perlite. Add 1 teaspoon of crushed eggshell for each three-inch pot, as African Violets need lots of lime.

Water   This is a plant which likes to be moist, but let it get *almost* dry before watering again. If dried out too much though, the roots will die and not take up water at the next watering. Leaves will droop like limp velvet. Roots and underground stem will rot right up to the soil line. Almost the same thing will happen if you overwater! So keep in the middle between sopping wet and bone dry.

Food   Being a blooming plant, use a high middle number fertilizer such as 5-8-7. Feed the plant every week.

Pests   Mealy bugs can settle under the closely growing leaves. Keep a watch on the underside of all the leaves, and immediately remove any white spots with rubbing alcohol on a Q-tip. Then wipe off all the leaves with rubbing alcohol.

Trimming   This is a nontrimming plant, as there is no central stem. Just be sure that you remove any limp or dead leaves from the bottom row. Repot when the center "neck" gets too long.

Starting New Plants   The leaves come up from the ground in a rosette. This means that they grow from the same underground center source. The plant can be propagated by seeds, but the new plants will be quite different from the one you have. Seeds do not grow plants "true" to the mother plant.

The only way to get the same plant variety is to grow from leaves. See Chapter 8, Method Two for complete directions.

ALUMINUM PLANT

Pilea cadierei

Then there is a plant with striped leaves, which comes from the moist warm area of Indo-China. It is known as the Aluminum Plant because of the broad stripes of green and shining aluminum color that run the full length of the leaves. The two- to three-inch-long leaves are oval and crisp-looking. They grow up the stem, alternating. The stems are light green and almost transparent. This is not a big plant, growing only about ten or twelve inches high.

Light   Grow the Aluminum Plant in a west or east window about a foot away from the windowpane, as it does not like too much sun. A north window is fine as long as the room is warm. Too much light will bleach the leaves.

Soil   This jungle plant prefers to grow in a rich soil-less mix. Use formula 3-2-1 of peat moss, vermiculite, and perlite.

Water   Look at the stems of this plant which are smooth and stiff, but look almost watery. This often suggests a plant which grows near a brook, or on the edge of a wet bog. So keep the soil moist, but the pot should not sit in a saucer full of water.

Food   Feed the plant an even-numbered formula, such as 20-20-20, or a similar even set of numbers.

Pests   This is a plant that seems to be bug-free as a general rule. It might once in a while get spider mite though, if the pest is loose in the plant's area.

Trimming   If the Aluminum Plant is not trimmed, it just grows straight up as a spindly stem with a cluster of leaves on top. At this stage it looks underfed and pathetic. Start trimming when the plant is quite small, and it will branch out and the center stem will grow thicker.

Starting New Plants   Plant stem cuttings in vermiculite following directions in the beginning of Chapter 8, under Method One.

CACTUS

Mammillaria dioica and *Cephalocereus senilis*

Maybe you are afraid that you'll forget to water your plant, and it will die. In this case, try one of the many members of the Cactus family. Or grow a cactus anyway just because there are so many strange and exciting shapes. Some are ridged, others have smooth barrels, and some have long white hair covering the long green cucumber shapes. But all have spines growing out of little tufts of white fuzz called *aureoles*. Try a *Mammillaria dioica* from Lower California which is long and fat and spiny. Or try the Old Man Cactus, *Cephalocereus senilis,* from Mexico, which is the one covered with long hair, like an all-over white beard.

Light   Put this in a south, west, or east window. It grows wherever you have the strongest, brightest light.

Soil   Cactus plants of all varieties prefer a very lean, gritty mix. Put together a 1-2-2 formula of peat moss, vermiculite, and perlite. You can substitute bird gravel for the vermiculite, or use half vermiculite and half bird gravel.

Water   Plants in this family are an extreme case in regard to water. They are kept almost bone-dry most of the year. In the summer, though, water very lightly once a week. If they get too much water, the whole plant will turn mushy overnight. These are plants which grow in our southwestern deserts. The rains come in the spring, and the soil stays moist, way down deep, during the summer. Then fall and winter are cool and dry, and the plant gets only dew at night. You might try a very light misting once a week in the winter.

Food   During the growing season, which is late spring into the middle of fall, give the plant a very, very light solution of 20-20-20 fertilizer, two or three times during this period.

Pests Cactus has been known to get mealy bugs among the spines. So watch the plants carefully.

Trimming Neither of these two plants can be trimmed, as they are each a self-contained barrel with no leaves or branches.

Starting New Plants There is no way to propagate these plants except by seeds. Some varieties will grow young plants at the base. These will develop roots, and can be cut away from the mother plant. Let these *pups* stay in a dry place for two or three weeks until the cut heals. A thin skin will form over the cut area to prevent rotting. Then plant the cactus in very dry, gravelly soil. Do not water until the plant shows signs of growth. Instead spray it lightly with water.

CHINESE BEAN SPROUTS

Mung Beans *Vigna radiata*

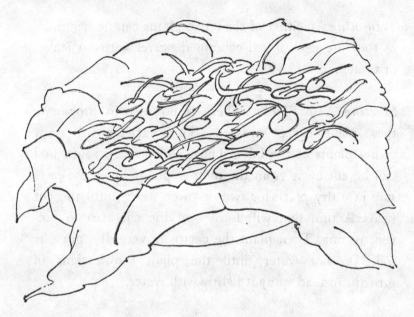

Some indoor plants are just for eating and also fun to grow. You get quick crop results, too! Chinese Bean Sprouts are grown from Mung Beans. These are planted in a shallow container and kept moist. In two or three days the inch-long white sprouts have grown out of the beans. Harvest, cook, and enjoy. They have a fresh, vegetable flavor and are crisp and crunchy. Stir them into soup, or mix with vegetables and meat, fry them with rice, or put them in a sandwich with cream or cottage cheese.

Light Put these in a west, east, or north window, as the beans need only enough light to make them sprout.

Soil They need *no soil*. See the next paragraph for growing instructions.

Water The beans will sprout in water. First line a shallow container with cheesecloth which overlaps the side. Spread the beans over the surface. Fill the dish with enough water to cover the beans, and let them soak overnight. Lift up the cheesecloth and beans and pour off the water. Replace them in the container. Then twice a day cover the beans with water and drain off immediately. After three or four days you can harvest your sprouts.

Food This planting will not develop leaves, so no fertilizer is needed.

Bugs You'll be eating the sprouts before any pests know they are around.

Trimming The only trimming you'll do is when you scoop out the sprouts to eat them.

Starting New Plants Just plant more beans for the next crop.

COLEUS or FLAME NETTLE
Coleus blumei

Would you like to own a plant with leaves so brightly colored that it doesn't need flowers to attract attention? Then get a Flame Nettle, a plant which is often just called by its Latin name of Coleus. It comes from Java, and other varieties grow in Africa, Madagascar, and India. The leaves are egg-shaped and a little jagged on the edges. Each leaf is brightly colored in patterns

of several shades of red with either green or yellow—
and sometimes all three colors. No two plants seem to
have exactly the same leaf patterns. It has a narrow
cluster of small, light-blue tube flowers on the end of
a stem.

Light Put the plant in a south window, as it likes lots
of sun. A west or an east window is the next choice. In
the summer, it will grow outside in a sunny part of the
garden.

Soil Use a light but rich 2-1-1 formula of peat moss,
vermiculite, and perlite. In the outside garden make
sure the soil is not stony and hard.

Water This plant needs water because of its large,
soft leaves and habit of growing rapidly. Make sure the
soil never dries out. In the winter, also spray the plant
with water once a day. Or, put the pot on an upturned
saucer in a tray of water. This way the plant will not
be standing in water, but the air around it will be
damp, as the water evaporates.

Food Because of its rapid growth, be sure to feed this
plant every week. Use the even-numbered formula of
20-20-20. If the leaves start to brown around the edges,
switch to a fertilizer with a high last number.

Pests White fly will settle on the plant. It often comes
along with the plant from the store or greenhouse. So

check it carefully when you buy it. At the first sign of any eggs or flies on the leaves, start washing with detergent and water. See Chapter 6 for full directions.

Trimming   If the Coleus is not trimmed, it will grow up with a single stem, losing leaves along the way. If you start trimming off the top leaves and stem when the plant is five or six inches high, the result will be a sturdy, bushy plant, glowing with color.

Starting New Plants   Once your plant is bushy, let one or two branches grow long, so that you can take cuttings to start new plants. Follow directions in the beginning of Chapter 8, under Method One. You can also buy seeds and start an assortment of plants of different color combinations. Follow directions in Chapter 8, Method Six for planting seeds and growing them into plants.

DIEFFENBACHIA

Dieffenbachia picta roehrsii and *Dieffenbachia picta superba*

Many varieties of Dieffenbachia have come from Central and South America. Some of the plants grow up to two feet tall, others will take off for the ceiling with leaves two feet long. The leaves are usually medium to light green, oval in shape, with white or ivory lines, splashes, and splotches in the center. They are very striking and tropical-looking, as if they were designed by an artist. Two good small varieties are *Dieffenbachia picta roehrsii*, and *Dieffenbachia picta superba*. You cannot always be sure which variety will be in the store or greenhouse, so pick out the one you like best. They are all good plants to grow in the house.

Light Dieffenbachia can be placed in a west or east window, but place the plant one to two feet away from the light. A north window is very good also.

Soil These plants grow best in the 1-1-1 combination of peat moss, vermiculite, and perlite. Start small plants in plastic pots. Once they start to grow taller, move to a clay pot for balance to prevent the plant from tipping over.

Water Most varieties do not like to be too wet. Water, then let the soil almost dry out, then water again. But don't water so much that the saucer fills up. If you give it too much water, the plant will let you know. Small drops will form around the edges of the leaves as the plant gets rid of the extra water.

Food The very green leaves will not turn yellow on the edges if you feed the plant with a high third number fertilizer, 7-6-19. It may once in a while need a sprinkling of chelated iron on the surface of the soil if the leaves become too light a green.

Pests Can get spider mite if the plant is not washed off once a week. You may find springtails on the top of the soil when you water the plant. Follow the directions in the beginning of Chapter 6 for getting rid of them.

Trimming This plant has only a tall center stem which never branches. The leaves cluster at the top as the plant grows taller. Even if the top is cut off, the plant will not branch, but it may send up new shoots from the bottom.

Starting New Plants A Dieffenbachia is an ideal plant for air-layering. Once this plant has grown tall it will look sort of scrawny. Follow the directions in Chapter 8 under Method Four.

A special bonus of plants may be grown from the rest of the stem, once the air-layering has developed roots and the top has been cut off and planted.

Cut the rest of the stem up into three- or four-inch lengths, depending on how long it is and how thick. Leave about three inches still attached to the original root in the pot. Throw the pieces into a plastic bag with enough damp, coarse sphagnum moss to partially cover them. Close the bag and hang it up in a low-light area. After a while, when you have almost forgotten about them, the pieces of stem will have developed roots. Pot up the lengths.

The original plant, too, may start sending up new shoots around the three-inch stump you left in the pot. This is really a cut-and-come-again plant.

MUSTARD AND CRESS

Brassica alba and *Lepidium sativum*

Another quick-growing-and-eating crop is formed from two types of seeds planted together. This is a great English favorite and is used in a sandwich in place of lettuce. As soon as the first two or three leaves are up, the inch-tall plants are cut with scissors and eaten.

Light Place the seeds in a south, west, or east window, as long as there is light enough to start them growing.

Soil   This indoor crop is harvested almost as soon as it is up. The soil-less mix is only used to hold the seeds and water and first roots. Use the basic 1-1-1 mix of peat moss, vermiculite, and perlite. Fill a wide, shallow container. This can be a clay or plastic plant saucer, or a one- to two-inch-deep cake pan. The seeds of cress are planted first on one-half of the surface. In four days they will have sprouted two green leaves. Then plant the mustard seeds on the rest of the surface. In two days they will be up. Two or three days later the whole affair will be one-inch high. Then harvest your crop with scissors.

Water   Use just enough water to moisten the soil. Too much will rot out the seeds, or float the roots of the seedlings right out of the soil. Add any water at the very edge of the container, so as not to disturb seeds or seedlings.

Food   No fertilizer is needed as the food contained in the seeds is all that is needed.

Bugs   There is no time for the plant to attract pests.

Trimming   The only trimming is when you harvest your one-inch-high crop.

Starting New Plants   No propagation from the plants. Just sow new seeds for the next crop.

PALM

Chamaedorea and *Howea kentia*

For the feel of a tropical island get a small Palm tree and watch it grow. There are several types of palms. Among them are: *Chamaedorea elegans* from Mexico, and *Howea kentia* from the Lord Howe Islands in the Pacific Ocean. These are not hard to grow, stay small, and are easy to find in the stores. The leaves are dark green and feathery. Leaves drop off the plant as the plant grows taller, so you will always have a stem marked with lighter-colored rings, and a cluster of leaves at the top. The *Howea* will bloom after it is three or four years old.

Light   Surprisingly enough, palm trees which bring to mind South Pacific Islands or jungles do not need a lot of light indoors. Perhaps this is because the young palm trees are sheltered by larger trees, so they do not get direct sunlight. And you are growing young trees in your garden. Put your Palm tree about two feet back from the windowpane in a south, west, or east window.

Soil   A 1-1-1 soil-less mix of peat moss, vermiculite, and perlite is just right for this plant.

Water   Like many tropical plants, the Palm likes to be kept moist. It can survive a drying out, but not too often. It likes to be misted with water.

Food   Feed it an even-numbered formula of 20-20-20 fertilizer. If the leaves start to yellow a bit, change to a high first number formula.

Pests   Scale often attacks this plant. If you see sticky spots on the upper sides of any leaves, look on the bottoms of the leaves above. If you find small, shiny light-brown spots, you know that's scale. To get rid of this pest, follow the directions in Chapter 6.

Trimming   A Palm cannot be trimmed, as it does not ever develop branches. It is always a straight-stemmed plant with a bunch of leaves at the top, except for one or two cluster palms.

Starting New Plants   There is no way to start a new plant from an old one. Palms are grown from seed. As a fun project you might try planting seeds from unpasteurized or fresh dates. These will sprout and you'll have single narrow leaves coming up from the center of the pot as the beginning leaves of a Palm called *Phoenix dactylifera*. It will be several years before the true palm fronds develop. Look in Chapter 8, Method Six for directions on planting seeds.

PIGGYBACK PLANT

Tolmiea menziesii

On this plant, the added attraction is that plantlets grow
right out of the leaves. This is the reason for the several
nicknames—Piggyback Plant, Pickaback Plant, Mother-
of-Thousands—for this plant, which grows naturally from
Alaska to California. The fresh green leaves look some-
what like maple tree leaves, with a few white, bristly
hairs on the surface. Hang the pot in a sunny window,
and the stems will grow and hang down. You'll soon
be potting up new plants for all your friends.

Light   Hang this plant in a west or east window, so it will only get bright light for half a day. It doesn't like too much sun.

Soil   The Piggyback does not need super-rich soil, so plant it in a 1-1-1 mix of peat moss, vermiculite, and perlite. Mix in a little lime in the form of ground egg-shells.

Water   Keep it moist. Being a hanging plant, it will drink more water than a regular plant. In addition, if you can mist it once a day, all the better.

Food   Feed with an even-numbered fertilizer, such as 20-20-20.

Pests   It is fairly free of any bugs. If there is any white fly around, it might settle on the leaves, so check them just to be sure. If you see either the eggs or flying crea-tures, follow directions in Chapter 6, to get rid of them.

Trimming   The leaf stalks grow up from the center so the plant will just get bushy as the pot fills with stalks. You need only trim off leaves that have turned brown and dry.

Starting New Plants   Cut off the stalk and the mother leaf with its plantlet. Stick the stalk in vermiculite up to the base of the leaf. When the plantlet gets larger, repot. See Chapter 8, Method Two for full details.

POLKA DOT or FRECKLE-FACE PLANT

Hypoestes sanguinolenta

Can you imagine green leaves covered with pink freckles? It's not a make-believe, comic-strip plant, or a magic, fairy-tale one. It's for real! The soft green, heart-shaped leaves are covered with pink spots, giving it the nicknames of Polka-Dot or Freckle-Face Plant. The plant can grow up to two feet high, with pairs of leaves which alternate in direction up the stem. Because it comes from Madagascar, it grows best in a warm room, but does not need bright sunlight. The flowers are small and pale lavender in color.

Light A west or east window is best. A south window is too bright, and a north one is not bright enough.

Soil Mix up your best rich soil-less mixture. Mix up formula 3-2-1 of peat moss, vermiculite, and perlite.

Water Do not allow this plant to dry out. Keep the soil moist, but not soggy. Drying out too much will make the thin leaves droop, and some may never recover.

Food Use an even-numbered food formula. Pick 20-20-20 or a similar even set of numbers.

Pests This plant can get spider mite, so wash it well all year around, once a week. It can also attract white fly if that pest is brought into the house on another plant.

Trimming This plant has even more problems than most, with its thin stems. The leaves seem too heavy for the stems, and grow thickly. But if it is trimmed when very small, it will branch out into a sturdy plant.

Starting New Plants No special tricks in making cuttings. Follow the clear directions at the beginning of Chapter 8 under Method One.

PRAYER PLANT

Maranta leuconeura kerchoviana

If you want a plant that moves, then the Prayer Plant is for you. You can recognize it by the dark brown pattern on the long, oval, light-green leaves. The pattern looks a bit like small, splashy leaves up the center vein of each leaf. (There are several plants which look like this, with different leaf patterns.) At night, the stems of the leaves move upright from an elbow-like joint. This goes on until all the leaves are standing upright, facing each other. It is a warm-growing plant from Brazil. It spreads along the ground in the jungle, so needs only a soft light.

Light　Put the plant in a west or east window, but back from direct sunlight. A north window is a very good choice as well.

Soil　This is a rich-soil plant, as are so many of the jungle floor coverings. Mix up the 3-2-1 formula of peat moss, vermiculite, and perlite.

Water　The Prayer Plant spreads its leaves wide during the day to keep moisture around its roots. Keep it moist in the pot. Do not let it dry out.

Food　Use the high first number fertilizer, as this plant needs nitrogen to keep its leaves green. If they begin to show yellow on the edges, switch to a high third number, 7-6-19.

Pests　It seems to be pretty free of pests. Like all plants in the dry air of the house, it might attract some spider mites. A few good washings will take care of this problem.

Trimming　It has no real center stem, and the plant takes care of its own flat branching effect by sending out clusters of leaves from the base.

Starting New Plants There is no center stem on the Prayer Plant. The leaf clusters come up directly from the soil. When the pot gets overfull, transplant. In transplanting, pull the plant apart gently with your hands. Depending on the size of the plant, break it up into two or three plants. Pot each one separately. See Chapter 8, and follow the directions described in Method Five.

PURPLE VELVET PLANT

Gynura aurantiaca

What about a purple plant. Purple? Yes, and its nicknames are Purple Velvet Plant and Chinese Velvet
Plant. Its home is Java, where the weather is warm,
and the sun bright. The leaves are about three inches
long and notched on the sides. They are very dark
green and covered with purple hairs like velvet or plush

cloth. The backs of the leaves are a deep red-purple. If you let the stems grow long, they will fall over the sides of the pot, two feet or more. The light shining on the hanging stems brings out the spectacular color. The flowers are not the color you might expect—they are a bright, fuzzy orange!

Light   South, west, or east windows are all ideal for this hanging plant.

Soil   Grow it in a rich, soil-less mix. Use formula 3-2-1 of peat moss, vermiculite, and perlite.

Water   It likes to be kept moist. If you decide to let the stems grow into long streamers, the plant will use up quantities of water. The larger the plant grows, the more water it will need.

Food   Being a dark-leaved plant, it can be fed with either a 20-20-20 food or one with a high first number which is nitrogen.

Pests   Count your blessings, as this seems to be a plant that does not attract bugs of any kind. Once in a great while it might get a mealy bug among its hairs but only if you have quantities of mealy bugs on other plants. And this should never happen!

Trimming   This is a natural hanging plant, but several plants in a pot can be kept at an eight- to ten-inch height by trimming the tops and keeping the branched effect. When you let the plants grow longer, still keep trimming. Instead of long, skinny stems with scattered leaves, you will have thickly branched stems. With eight or so of these stems falling over the edge of a pot, the red-purple color is startling. They will trail down as long as two to three feet.

Starting New Plants This a hanging plant, so it will have long pieces to be trimmed off. The leaves alternate along the center stem. There is usually a tight cluster of four or five leaves at the end. Do not count this set of leaves, but cut the stem between the fourth and fifth leaf below the top cluster. Cut off just one leaf (the fourth) and add rooting powder to the end of stem and cut leaf area. Put into the vermiculite, covering the cut leaf area. Follow the rest of the suggestions in Method One at the beginning of Chapter 8, for rooting and potting the cutting.

RED-NERVED FITTONIA
Fittonia verschaffeltii

Another pink-and-green plant is Red-Nerved Fittonia. It is a low and sprawling plant from South America. The four-inch-long, oval leaves spread flat, showing the pattern of deep pink veins against dark green. It is a plant that grows along the ground in a warm jungle, so only needs a soft light. It is so colorful that one would not care whether it had flowers or not. It does, though, have tiny ones on a long spike.

There is also a white-veined type, the Silver-Nerved Fittonia, or *Fittonia argyroneura*. A new, tiny-leafed variety with white veins is called Dwarf Nerve Plant, or *Fittonia minor*, or *minima*.

Light Put it in a west or east window, but place the plant about a foot away from the window, so that direct sunlight will not fall on the leaves. A north window with unbroken light is also a good growing spot.

Soil This plant sprawls over the rich soil on the jungle floor. Give it the 3-2-1 formula of peat moss, vermiculite, and perlite.

Water As it grows on the jungle floor where the soil is moist and damp, the plant likes the same conditions indoors. Its leaves spread flat on the ground to help it hold moisture around its roots in case there is a dry spell in the jungle. Make sure it never gets a dry spell in the house.

Food Mix up a high first number fertilizer. But if you have only the even-numbered fertilizer, you can use that. Then, add a small amount of chelated iron to the top of the soil every two months to keep the leaves green and healthy.

Pests If leaves start yellowing, check for spider mites. If you've found them wash off the plant every few days to be sure the bugs are gone.

Trimming This is a creeping plant and if it is not trimmed back it will just grow along in a straight line. Eventually the single stem will flop over the edge of the pot and continue to grow hanging down. Trimming will force it to send out other runners. The surface of the soil will be covered then, and the plant will become a flat mass of red-veined green leaves.

Starting New Plants Let one of the running branches grow longer than the others. Trim it off and grow it into a new plant, following directions in Method One described in the beginning of Chapter 8.

ROSE or LEMON GERANIUM
Pelargonium

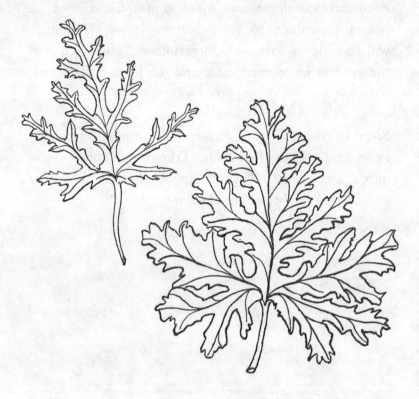

There are plants whose leaves smell like the flower or fruit of another plant such as Rose Geranium, or *Pelargonium graveolens* and *Pelargonium capitatum,* and Lemon Geranium, or *Pelargonium crispum* and *Pelargonium 'Dr. Livingston.'* These are just two of the named varieties which are rose- or lemon-scented, and there are other fragrances as well. Pick your plant by its scent, not by its name, as names change all over the place. The leaves are light green, and some look like deeply cut maple leaves, while others are lacy like snow-flakes. All of the Pelargoniums come from South Africa, and are sometimes called Storksbill because of the shape of the seed pod. These are florists' or greenhouse geraniums. The true geraniums or *Geraniaceae* are northern wildflower annuals called Cranesbill, after the seed pod shape.

Light   The scented geraniums grow in hot, dry places, so will grow well outdoors in the summer, and all year round in the house. Pick a south, west, or east window for bright light.

Soil   All geraniums can be potted in a soil almost like the one used for cactus, but not quite as gritty. Make the basic 1-1-1 mix of peat, vermiculite, and perlite, then add another half measure of bird gravel. The roots of geraniums like to work through stony soil.

Water   The plants come from semi-desert areas in Africa, but they need more water than cactus plants. Water them all year round. Let the soil dry out between waterings, then soak well. The roots and leaves will not suffer from this alternate drying out and soaking with water, as they are used to this treatment.

Food   Use a weak solution of even-numbered formula 20-20-20, or a similar one, about every two weeks.

Pests   All of the scented geraniums seem to be pest

free. If there are white flies in the house they will settle on the leaves, but not happily. Wash off with water and detergent following directions in Chapter 6.

Trimming The plants will be all the better for a good trimming. Keep them cut back to a foot or less in height. Odd branches then will start growing along the stem, as well as tufts of leaves. The stem will thicken, giving the effect of a gnarled tree trunk. As you trim, the room will be filled with the lovely scent of the leaves.

Starting New Plants Trim off the top or branches in the usual way. Take off the two lower leaves and dip the end of the stem in rooting powder. *But,* the cuttings are planted in an *almost* dry mixture of bird gravel, vermiculite, perlite, and plain potting soil (no humus) in equal quantities. Do not water unless the soil gets bone dry. But spray the stem and leaves, two or three times a day. These cuttings are among the most difficult to grow, so do not be discouraged if you lose a few.

SNAKE PLANT

Sansevieria trifasciata

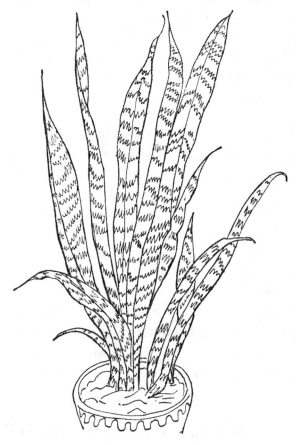

A foolproof plant is the Snake Plant. It comes from the warm partly dry Congo area, which gives you a hint on how to grow it. The long narrow leaves are very stiff, growing up from the soil with no stem at all. They are marked with dark-green, wavy, horizontal lines against a gray-white background. They grow very slowly, which is a good habit for an indoor plant.

Light Put the plant in the brightest sun you have. A south window is best if you have it. Otherwise pick a west or east window. It will also live in a north window, but the growth will be *very* slow.

Soil You can use the 1-1-1 formula of peat moss, vermiculite, and perlite for this plant. It prefers a richer soil than a cactus mixture.

Water Pour just enough water in the pot to moisten the soil, but not to make it soaking wet. Then let it almost dry out, and then water again. If it has to stay dry for a week or two, it will not die.

Food Feed very lightly every two weeks to a month with a 20-20-20 even-numbered formula.

Pests This plant never seems to get any pests, perhaps because the leaves are so hard and smooth. If there are mealy bugs loose in the house, one might snuggle down into the cracks between the leaves at the soil level. Check in there every so often for any white fluff that is not perlite.

Trimming As there is no center stem, and no branching, there is no way to trim this plant.

Starting New Plants Cut off a leaf for new plants. Take one from the outside, not the inside, of the cluster, as this might stop the plant from growing. Cut the leaf in two-inch sections crosswise. As you cut, lay the pieces flat on a sheet of paper in the original shape of the leaf. This way, the cut edge facing the roots is always "down." This is the edge that has to go into the soil. Root powder goes on this edge which is "buried" in the vermiculite about one-half inch deep. If you make a mistake and put the other edge of the cutting in the soil, the cutting will not grow. Follow directions in Chapter 8, Method Two on root-growing conditions, and potting up the final plantlet.

Or, if the plant develops new plants around it at the soil level, divide the whole group, and plant in separate pots. See Chapter 8, Method Five for full directions.

SPIDER PLANT

Chlorophytum elatum vittatum

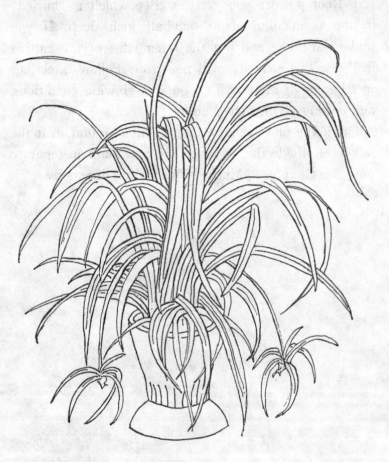

A Spider Plant is a foolproof one to grow. The long, thin leaves have a white stripe down the middle. They curve up from the soil level without any center stem. A long runner curves out from the middle of a bunch of leaves. Tiny, white lily flowers form at the end, and when they drop off, a small plantlet will develop.

This makes a beautiful hanging plant. It will look like a green and white fountain with small plants hanging down around the edges of the pot.

Light Grow in either a south, west, or east window, but place the plant about a foot from the windowpane. It will also grow in a north window. Lower light sometimes helps the plant to bloom, which means more plantlets.

Soil An even formula of 1-1-1 of peat moss, vermiculite, and perlite is best. Put the soil and the plant in a hanging pot, or one that can be hung when the plantlets start dropping over the side on their runners.

Water Somehow you can never give a Spider Plant too much water. As a hanging plant it grows plantlets on long stems and these absorb water. The mother plant's roots are drinking up water for both plant and plantlets. So keep it moist, and never let it dry out.

Food This plant will do well with the even-numbered food formula 20-20-20. The ends of the leaves often turn brown and dry though. A high first and third number formula may help this condition, so try a 7-6-19 fertilizer.

Pests The Spider Plant does not seem to attract any pests.

Trimming The pot is filled with long single leaves hanging in clusters over the edge. Trimming them has no effect on the plant, as there is no center stem.

Starting New Plants The long flowering stalks develop plantlets on the end after blooming. New plants are started by pinning down the plantlets in another pot, while they are still attached to the mother plant. Read the complete directions for this type of propagating in Chapter 8 under Method Three.

Also, when the mother plant gets too large for its pot you can break up the roots into chunks for new plants. This is also described in Chapter 8 under Method Five.

STRAWBERRY GERANIUM

Saxifraga stolonifera (sarmentosa)

The Strawberry Geranium comes from China and it is neither a strawberry nor a geranium plant! To make things ever more confusing it is also called Strawberry Begonia, Magic Carpet, or Mother-of-Thousands. So my advice is, memorize the real name, *Saxifraga stolonifera,* and you'll always get what you want.

It is a tiny, creeping plant with round, dark-green

leaves that are red underneath. It sends out long, thin runners at ground level. Small plants develop at the ends of the runners. They can be planted in new pots to start new plants.

Light   Put it in the south, west, or east window for full light.

Soil   Coming from a cool mountain area, it does not demand the rich jungle-type soil. Mix up the basic formula of 1-1-1 of peat moss, vermiculite, and perlite.

Water   This plant is not used to too much water, and gets a good deal of moisture from mountain morning fogs. So let it almost dry out between waterings, then soak.

Food   An even-numbered food is best for this plant, so use a 20-20-20 formula.

Pests   This hairy plant can attract mealy bugs, so lift up all leaves and look under them if they look droopy. Also remove all dead leaves from the soil surface, as bugs can hide under them.

Trimming   The Strawberry Geranium is a small ground-cover plant without a center stem.

Starting New Plants   Runners spread out from the center of the plant, with plantlets on the ends. Pin down the plantlets as described in Chapter 8, Method Three.

SWEDISH IVY

Plectranthus australis

If you would like a plant sold under a false nickname get Swedish Ivy. It is not an ivy, and does not come from Sweden, but from Australia and Africa. The bright, shiny leaves are round, and saw-toothed on the edges. In some varieties, the leaves are covered with fine hairs, others are purple underneath. It can be grown as a hanging plant, or kept trimmed back to grow over the surface of a wide, shallow pot. Pale blue flowers cluster tightly together at the top of a stalk. There are several named varieties, but *australis* is the best.

Light   This is a good plant for a west or east window, as it does not like too much sun.

Soil   A well-balanced soil-less mix of 1-1-1 peat moss, vermiculite, and perlite will keep this plant growing well.

Water   Keep the soil damp, but not soaking wet. Remember, when it reaches hanging length it will need more water.

Food   Pick out an even-numbered formula, like 20-20-20, to feed the plant.

Pests   Because the leaves lie close together, mealy bugs may settle in during the warm, damp days of August. Check the plant during the year, and especially during the summer, for those, telltale, sticky, white spots.

Trimming   The plant should be well trimmed if you want it to stay flat on the surface of the soil. Let it grow if you want a hanging plant. Once the stems start hanging over the edge, trim each one back a bit to keep them bushy, and an even length all round.

Starting New Plants   Allow the hanging stems to get a little long, then trim off and use these ends as cuttings to start new plants. Follow directions in Chapter 8, Method One.

WANDERING JEW

Tradescantia fluminensis and *Tradescantia blossfeldiana*
'*Variegata*'

Wandering Jew is a trailing plant from Argentina. The
first variety has small, bright-green leaves which are

purple-violet underneath. The second variety has dark-green, hairy leaves striped with silver-white, and they are purple underneath. There are many other combinations of greens, whites, purples, and reds. Both leaves and stems are crisp. Stems will wander over the edge of a pot and hang down.

Light   This is a plant which does well in a west, east, or even a north window. It does not like too bright a light. The leaves can be burned by hot sun, turn brown, and dry up.

Soil   A soil-less mix formula of 2-1-1 of peat moss, vermiculite, and perlite should be used.

Water   Keep this plant moist but not overwet. Let the soil in the pot dry a bit before watering again. You will have to check the amount of water needed, as it varies. If it is growing in a north window it will not need as much water. There will be no sun to evaporate the water from the soil, through heat. In a west or east window more water will be needed.

Food   An even-numbered formula such as 20-20-20 is used.

Pests   This one is fairly bug-proof, but if the room gets too dry the plant may be attacked by spider mite. Spray the plant every other day to keep its leaves moist. If it does get any pests, follow the treatment described in Chapter 6.

Trimming Trimming is necessary to keep this plant from growing long, scraggly stems. You will want a bushy plant with healthy stems and leaves hanging over the sides of the pot.

Starting New Plants The stems root easily, and you can use your trimmings to start new plants. Follow directions given in Chapter 8, Method One. Some people put the stems in water to start new plants. This can be done, but the roots will be weak. The new plants will not grow as well as those started in vermiculite.

MARIGOLD
Tagetes

The Marigold is a native of the area from New Mexico to Argentina. The flowers are a mass of curly petals in glowing yellow, or orange, or mixed orange and red-brown. The leaves are finely cut almost like coarse fern leaves, but small. The plants range in size from the eight-inch Dwarf or French marigolds, to the large ones thirty inches high, whose flowers are three inches across. The variety names change from seed house to seed house, and from year to year. Pick out the size and color you want and see what happens. Any left-over seed can be planted indoors in the fall to grow and flower indoors in the winter.

Light   The sunniest part of the outdoor garden is best for marigolds. As a houseplant it can be put in the south, west, or east window, but south is the best of all, as it has the strongest sun.

Soil   Prepare the soil in your garden according to directions in Chapter 3. Wait until the soil is warm enough for seed planting. If you put in plants, wait until all chance of cold nights has gone. Inside, plant seeds in vermiculite, and transplant to a 1-1-1 mix of peat moss, vermiculite, and perlite. See Chapter 8, Method Six for a full description of seed planting.

Water   Outside, use a fine spray in watering, as seeds and seedlings are easily washed out of the ground. As the plants grow larger, water whenever the soil dries out. The amount naturally depends on rainstorms, cloudy weather, and hot sunny days. Water between the rows so as not to wash soil away from the roots. When putting in plants instead of seeds, soak the plant roots well as they go into the soil. When growing indoors, keep the plants moist, but not soaking wet.

Food Use a 5-10-10 dry mixture of fertilizer worked into the soil before planting. After the plants are growing, add a thin dusting of fertilizer to the soil between the rows of plants. Be careful not to get it on the plants themselves. Rake it into the top surface. When the plants begin to flower, add a thin covering of fertilizer between the rows, and again rake it into the soil.

For inside growing, pick a 5-8-7 formula, as marigolds are blooming plants and you'll want a high second number.

Pests Marigolds will get aphids unless the seed has been treated. Red spiders are also a threat. Follow directions in Chapter 6 for the right cure.

Trimming Trim when the plants are very small, so that branching will start early. The more branches, the more flowers. Once flower buds show, let the plant bloom, then trim again.

Starting New Plants When these are grown indoors, you can propagate new plants from cuttings in the usual way, by following directions in Chapter 8, Method One. These new plants will develop much quicker than those grown from seed.

PETUNIA

Solanaceae

Petunia belongs to a family with as mixed a set of rela-
tives as you're liable to find. This family includes pota-
toes, tomatoes, eggplant, red pepper, tobacco, and
many, many more. The Petunia originally came from
South America, and likes a hot, sunny summer. The
flowers are white, many shades of pink and red, and
light and dark blue. There are ruffled edges and plain
edges, and patterns of red-and-white, and blue-and-
white. The trumpet-shaped flowers are faintly sweet,

and the leaves are soft and sticky. Choose your seeds from a wide variety in a seed catalog, or a rack in a local plant store.

Light   Plant these in the brightest part of the garden, or in a window box which gets good light. Indoors, pick a south, west, or east window.

Soil   The seeds need warm soil with all the frost out of the ground, and no chance of a cold snap. Plants go into the soil much later than seeds, when the air is warm. See Chapter 3 for description of how to prepare outdoor soil. For indoor growing use a 1-1-1 formula of peat moss, vermiculite, and perlite.

Water   Follow the directions for watering described under Marigold.

Food   Petunias need the same fertilizer as marigolds, so follow the same directions.

Pests   They seem to be free of pests.

Trimming   Trim back early in order to strengthen the plant. The more branches, the more flowers.

Starting New Plants   New plants can be propagated indoors from cuttings in the usual way. Follow directions given in Chapter 8, Method One. For seeding, follow directions in Chapter 8, Method Six.

TOMATO

Lycopersicon esculentum and *Lycopersicon pimpinelli-folium*

If you want to eat the fruit of a plant, then a Tomato is a perfect choice. Originally it came from South America, and is in the Nightshade family, *Solanaceae.*

There are small- and large-size plants and fruits. Try Patio for portable containers outdoors. Beefsteak or Rutgers are good for large plants in the garden. Tiny Tim is good for indoor window-sill growing. The leaves are all medium-green with irregular cuts, and are sort of hairy and sticky. If you rub the leaves they will stain your fingers a yellow-green, and leave behind their own sharp green-tomato smell. All the plants have tiny, lemon-yellow flowers.

Light   This plant needs good bright light outdoors. Inside, a sunny window facing south is best.

Soil   Plants usually go into warm outdoor soil around the end of May. See Chapter 3 for full directions on preparing outdoor soil. Indoors use a 2-1-1 soil-less mix of peat moss, vermiculite, and perlite.

Water   Plants in the garden should be well separated, not in rows, so they are watered separately. Soak well when first planted. Then keep moist around the roots, watering when the soil first begins to look dry. Judge this by rainstorms and hot sun. These are fleshy plants needing lots of water and hot sun. Indoors, keep the soil moist.

Food   Often, dried cow manure is mixed with the soil at the bottom of the hole into which the plant is put. Water is added over the roots and the roots are covered with soil. Use a dry 5-10-10 mixture after the plant is growing well, and when it starts to bud.

Pests Plants attract aphids as well as white flies, so wash off leaves with detergent and water.

Trimming Trimming is done early to keep the plants bushy. Then as the plant grows, trim off the "suckers," which are the thin stems which grow between the main stem and the real branch. This will help produce more flowers, therefore more tomatoes.

Starting New Plants Branches or leaves are far apart on the stems, making it hard to take small-size cuttings. It is best to plant seeds. Seeds are planted indoors for both outdoor and indoor plants. See Chapter 8, Method Six for full directions.

Special Tip When growing tomatoes indoors, you will have to shake the plant once it develops flowers. This takes the place of the outside wind and bees. The pollen then reaches the stigma inside the flower, and tomatoes start to form.

ZINNIA

Crassina

Also from Mexico and South America is the Zinnia.
There are too many sizes, colors in the red, yellow, and
orange tones, plus flower forms and hybrid names, to
list a particular plant variety. There are miniature,
standard, or mammoth plants. You're on your own.
Miniatures are from four to fourteen inches high, and
are the best for small gardens. Those mammoth twenty-
four-inch-high plants will have to be held up with
wooden supports. Leaves are medium-green, stiff and
rough. Petals of the flowers are also stiff and crisp,

overlapping each other from a center into a half-round head.

Light A sunny garden area is the best. For indoors, pick a south window, as it's the lightest, with west or east as a second choice.

Soil Prepare the garden soil, following the directions in Chapter 3. Just be sure it is warm enough for the seeds of this half-hardy annual. Plants go into the ground much later than seeds. For indoor growing, use a soil-less 1-1-1 mix of peat moss, vermiculite, and perlite.

Water Follow the Marigold directions for both outdoor and indoor watering.

Food Feed this plant the same as you would feed a Marigold.

Pests This plant will get spider mites, so keep the plants well washed.

Trimming Zinnias will branch as the result of a good trimming. They will also develop a stronger stem so the plant will not fall over, as well as more flowers.

Starting New Plants These are a little hard to propagate from cuttings, as the leaves are far apart on the stems. For seeding, follow directions in Chapter 8, Method Six.

Chapter 11

GOING ON VACATION

What do you do with your plant pet when you go away on vacation?

There is no problem if your whole family is going together to a house in the country or seashore. Then you can take your plant with you.

Find a cardboard box that is wide enough to hold the pot, and deep enough to hold the pot and plant. The closed top of the box should be at least three inches above the top leaves of the plant. If you are leaving in the morning, pack your plant the night before. If you leave late in the afternoon, do your packing during the day.

First, give the plant a good watering before putting it in the box. Put a close-fitting saucer in first, so the box will not absorb water from the soil. Then set the plant in the middle of the box. Place a box of fertilizer in the box beside it.

Now stuff crumpled newspaper in the bottom of the box. Fill in the whole bottom as high as the top of the pot. The paper should press tightly around the pot, so it is held firmly and will not tip over.

At the last minute—or hour—put the top over the box and tie cord around box and top. Punch a few air holes on each side of the box.

When you put it in the car, be sure it is steady, and will not tip over. Do not put anything heavy on top of the box.

When you get to the vacation house, find the right window for your plant, and unpack it as soon as you can.

If you are going someplace where you will not be able to take your plant, ask someone at home to take care of your pet. Leave printed instructions beside the pot. Include directions on when to water and when to feed the plant, and how much. Put the fertilizer can beside the pot. If the plant is almost ready to repot, do this before you leave for the summer.

But what do you do if everyone is going away together for a two- or three-week vacation and you can't take your pet along or leave it with a friend?

If your pet is a cactus, then you don't have to worry. Give it a pat and say you'll be back soon. It will take care of itself, living off the water stored in its barrel.

Or, you can make a vacation home for your pet, and leave it alone in the room. How? It's simple.

The day before you leave the house, water the plant very well. Stand the pot in its saucer. Push four thin sticks into the soil at the edge of the pot. Angle them out a bit so the tips are above and outside the leaves of the plant.

Now put the saucer and pot into a plastic bag which is large enough to cover the plant, and be tied on top.

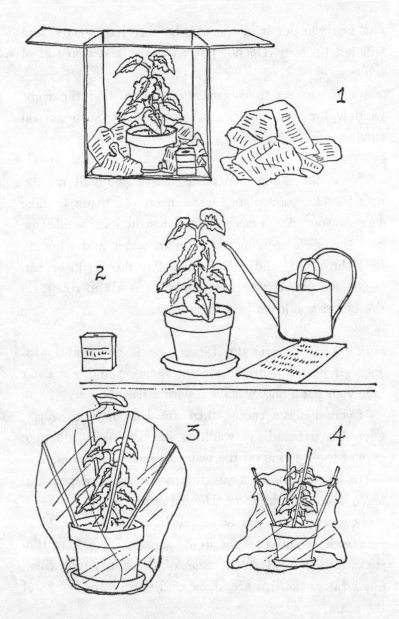

VACATION CARE. 1. View of plant inside carrying box; newspaper to pack around pot. 2. Box of fertilizer, plant, watering can, and a list of instructions for "friendly care." 3. Plant left at home in a plastic bag. 4. Slow opening of bag after you return home.

The sticks will keep the plastic from touching the leaves.

Bring the open edges of the bag together. Just before twisting and tying them together, blow into the bag as if you were blowing into a balloon. This, too, will keep the sides of the bag away from the leaves. Tie the top tightly, so air and the moisture in the pot will not escape.

Place the plant where it will have light, but where the *sun will not touch the plastic bag*. The sun, heating up the damp air inside the bag, will cook the plant. The leaves will turn into a gooey mound. Less light will keep the plant from growing too fast, so the water in the soil will not be used up. Moisture will evaporate from the leaves into the air in the bag. It will then be absorbed again by both the soil and the leaves. During this time the plant will not have to be fed.

You might want to try this out sometime as an experiment, to see how long the pot will keep its moisture, and how long the plant stays healthy. It's like growing plants in a terrarium.

When you get home, loosen the top of the bag just a little. Reach down and check the soil for moisture. Add water if needed. Do not take the bag off the plant immediately. It will have to get used to the outside room air, after having been in the humid air of the bag. Each day open the top of the bag a little bit more.

After about five days, slide the bag halfway down the plant. Hold it in place with pieces of sticky tape against the sticks. If the plant starts to droop after an hour, bring the bag up to the top of the sticks. Close the top a bit. But, if the plant is not affected by the room air, wait another day, then take the bag away completely. Put in its usual place.

CLOSING NOTE: ENJOY YOUR PET

You have now taken care of your plant pet under all conditions, and can boast of having a green thumb. Try all sorts of plants to see what happens with each one. You may lose a few, but everyone does, and you'll learn from your mistakes. Trade plants with friends. You'll soon find that you have an exciting collection of pets, all different, but each one beautiful to look at. The more plants you have, the easier it is to take care of them.

Who knows, someday you may have your own commercial greenhouse, or plant store. Until then, have fun growing plants and raising lots of house-loving pets.

SOURCES OF SUPPLIES

First look in the Yellow Pages under: Florists-Retail, Florists Supplies, Garden Supplies-Retail, Nurserymen, Plants-Retail. Also look for plants and supplies at local garden centers, variety stores, and supermarkets.

FERTILIZERS

Here are a few suggestions of brands. You'll find many others in your local stores. Atlas Fish Emulsion Fertilizer 5-1-1, Hyponex 7-6-19 (this brand also has other formulas), Stern's Miracid 30-10-10, Peters 20-20-20 (this brand also has other formulas), Stim-u-plant African Violet Food 5-8-7. Buy these wherever plant supplies are sold.

PLANTS

Buy these from your local stores, or greenhouses. You can order some plants by mail. First, send for catalogs which will list the plants and their prices.

Cactus

Abbey Garden, 176 Toro Canyon Road, Carpinteria, Calif. 93013

Henrietta's Nursery, 1345 N. Brawley, Fresno, Calif. 93705

Ed Storms, 4223 Pershing, Fort Worth, Tex. 76107

African Violets

Fischer Greenhouses, Linwood, N.J. 08221

Lyndon Lyon, Dolgeville, N.Y. 13329. List 10¢

Tinari Greenhouses, 2325 Valley Rd., Huntingdon Valley, Penna. 19006. List 25¢

Herbs

Caprilands Herb Farm, Coventry, Conn. 06238

Green Herb Gardens, Greene, R.I. 02827

Sunnybrook Herb Farm, Chesterfield, Ohio 44026. Catalog 25¢

Tropical Plants

Alberts & Merkel Bros., Boynton Beach, Fla. 33435

International Growers Exchange, P.O.B. 397, Farmington, Mich. 48024

Merry Gardens, Camden, Maine, 04843. List 25¢, Catalog $1.00

Geo. W. Park Seed Co., Greenwood, S.C. 29646

Tropical Paradise Greenhouse, 8825 W. 79th St., Overland Park, Kan. 66104

SEEDS

If you order seeds by mail, you have a better choice from a large catalog. A local store may have only a few varieties of seeds.

John Brudy's Rare Plant House, Box 84, Cocoa Beach, Fla. 32931 (tropical fruit trees)

W. Atlee Burpee, Philadelphia, Penna. 19132; Clinton, Iowa 52732; Riverside, Calif. 92504

Gurney Seed & Nursery Co., Yankton, S.D. 57078

Geo. W. Park Seed Co., Greenwood, S.C. 29646

Stokes Seeds, Box 548, Buffalo, N.Y. 14240

SUPPLIES BY MAIL ORDER

Vernard J. Greeson, 3548 N. Cramer St., Milwaukee, Wis. 53211. List 10¢

The House Plant Corner, Box 5000, Cambridge, Md. 21613

Geo. W. Park Seed Co., Greenwood, S.C. 29646

Fred A. Veith, 3505 Mozart Ave., Cincinnati, Ohio 45211

Index

VIRGINIE FOWLER ELBERT has been growing plants since she was eight years old, when her grandfather helped her plant her first garden. Now, living in an apartment on Manhattan's Upper West Side, she surrounds herself with many of the plants listed in this book. In fact, most of the plant portraits had living models.

In addition to gardening, Virginie Elbert enjoys pottery, enameling, shell collecting, and jewelry making. Formerly a juvenile book editor, she has combined her talents in writing numerous plant and craft books for both children and adults.